*Casting off*

# *Casting off*

A MEMOIR

Elspeth Sandys

OTAGO

*For my friends*

First published 2017


ISBN 978-0-947522-55-1

A catalogue record for this book is available from the National Library of New Zealand. 

Editor: Jane Parkin

Printed in China through Asia Pacific Offset

## Acknowledgements

My warm thanks to the Michael King Writers' Centre, and to Ka Meecham and Tania Stewart, for the two-month residency which enabled me to write this book.

I would also like to thank Rachel Scott for her loyalty and wise counsel, Gwynnedd Somerville for her loving involvement, and my friend Carole Angier for everything.

## Author's Note

This is an incomplete memoir. Out of respect for people close to me I have left large gaps. If anything in the book causes distress or gives offence, I am truly sorry. I make no claim for what I have written to be seen as The Truth. It is *my* truth, that is all.

'They change their sky, not their soul, who rush across the sea …
What you seek is here.'

'Caelum non animum mutant qui trans mare currunt.'

*The Odes of Horace*

# Chapter One

The name I answer to in 1956 is not my true name. Let's just say I'm the bad news my parents never wanted to hear.

I'm sixteen. Horrible age. I'm mutating, like a species of fish, from childhood to adulthood, an identity I have already adopted in a number of no doubt suspect ways. Three different homes and three different families – my adoptive father died when I was fourteen; my adoptive mother has been intermittently confined to mental hospital – have something to do with that. As has reading, anything and everything I can lay my hands on. My current craze is Graham Greene. *The End of the Affair* will haunt me through decades as turbulent as those Greene himself lived through. So, for different reasons, will Thackeray's *Vanity Fair*, Hardy's *Tess of the d'Urbervilles*, George Eliot's *Middlemarch*, and the shocking and sometimes silly novels of D.H. Lawrence. So far, post childhood, I've blasted my way through half a dozen Dickens novels, a fair dollop of Trollope, all of Hardy, *The Cruel Sea* (page 99 learned by heart), *For Whom the Bell Tolls*, *The Great Gatsby*, most of Forster and Eliot, and *Moby Dick*, not to mention a pre-teen passion for the novels of Georgette Heyer and an obsession with Shakespeare.

With so many different adult voices competing for attention in my head, is it any wonder I've become an expert in pretending I know what I'm talking about?

I'm sitting in the living room of my current home listening to the news on the radio. The announcer is talking about the possibility of a third world war. 1956 will go down in history as 'The Year of the Suez Crisis'. Or, if you want the official designation, 'The Year of the Tripartite (Britain, France and Israel, sitting in the naughty chairs) Aggression'. The family I'm living with – mother, father, two daughters – are all in the room with me. The atmosphere is solemn.

'I'm utterly convinced that the action we have taken is the right one,' the British prime minister, Anthony Eden, is saying. The mother of the family nods; the father frowns; the daughters – one the same age as me, the other two years younger – fiddle and look bored.

I'm fiddling too, but out of excitement not boredom. My fiddling always takes the same form. I spell out words on the back of my hand. I can't remember what words I spelt out as I listened to the honeyed voice of Great Britain's prime minister, but I'm sure they had something to do with my belief that the British – well, the English – always did the Right Thing. Staring up at me from the discarded newspaper on the floor is a photo of Anthony Eden at the door of Number 10. He's handsome. I picture him standing up to the Nazis, resisting their terrible tortures, embodying the spirit that won the war. Today he's talking about a new enemy, an Egyptian called Gamal Abdel Nasser, who has seized the Suez Canal from its rightful owners, the British. I feel indignation, outrage, anger. I have no doubt the military action my hero has taken is justified both morally and legally.

'Is there going to be war?' the younger of the sisters asks.

'Hush,' the mother answers. 'Listen.'

'Is there, Daddy?'

'Let's hope not, darling.'

Over the next few days as my Romantic Toryism (not a phrase I would have used in 1956) comes under fire from those who think differently, I grapple with emotions that have no fixed point of reference but are nevertheless invested with a power I can neither escape nor fully comprehend. The father of the family I'm living with isn't happy with Mr Eden's handling of the crisis. Neither are a lot of other people, including the American president. Mr Eden is married to a niece of Winston Churchill. Surely this guarantees his good faith? When he resigns two months after this first broadcast, anguish tears at my heart. In the photo printed in that morning's paper he looks like a man who has had all his fingernails pulled out. The report mentions, among other things, that at the height of the crisis he didn't sleep for three nights in a row.

How will he live now? What will become of him?

(Reading this passage some weeks later I'm suddenly gripped by doubt. Did this event happen in this way, in this place? Another image is shadowing that living room, those people, those words. I'm back in my legal home, sitting by the window of the room we called the 'breakfast room' – though no one ever ate breakfast there – and I'm listening to that exact same broadcast while my mother hovers threateningly in the background. Which memory is true? The one I have just described, or its shadow? Jenny Diski, in her brave and brilliant farewell to the world, *In Gratitude*, declared memoir to be 'a form that ... plays hide and seek with the truth. It contains what I imagine and what I remember being told'. So maybe neither memory is true. But what has clung to that occluded 'event', what I feel now when I think back, *that* is true.)

* * *

My Romantic Toryism persisted through my teens but with decreasing intensity. By the time I was twenty it had given way to more robust beliefs. But the tendency to see the best in people and in the causes I supported – to romanticise, in other words – remained, opening me up to the criticism (both then and now) of being naïve and other-worldly. But I never quite gave up my sympathy with the handsome prime minister (and his beautiful Churchillian wife) who so nearly took us into a third world war. Eden lived for another twenty years in what might be described as 'privileged obscurity'. But that doesn't answer the questions I asked as an anguished sixteen-year-old. How *did* Eden live with such a massive failure as his legacy? What becomes of a human being judged so harshly by history?

'All political lives … end in failure,' Enoch Powell, a very different kind of Tory, wrote in his biography of Joseph Chamberlain. 'That is the nature of politics and of human affairs.' So are we all doomed to failure? Is that what the brilliant but now discredited Powell was saying? Or is there another way to look at life's 'slings and arrows'? Anthony Eden called his memoir *Full Circle*. Who's to say he didn't find peace, even happiness, telling the story of the whole of his life, not just the ignominious end to his political career? 'Time present and time past / Are both perhaps present in time future / And time future contained in time past …' Eden was a literary man. T.S. Eliot's words, from *Burnt Norton*, written in 1935, over two decades before Suez, would almost certainly have been familiar to him. Even if they weren't, he would know as soon as he began to write his memoir that to tell a story about the past is to tell a story about the present and the future. It may be fashionable in 2017 to talk of closure, but I don't believe there is any such thing.

So this is a story of a life that starts in hope and ends in failure, as it was bound to, but refuses to make that the whole of the story. A life as mysterious as all lives are, lived in a particular time, in particular places, peopled by characters whose like we will never see again.

# Chapter Two

I am a fiction writer. This doesn't mean what I'm writing here will be fiction, though inevitably much of it will be. We don't remember facts except by accident or act of will (I can recite the capital cities of most European countries, but I don't pretend that helps me to live). What we remember are feelings, smells, touch, inconsistencies, ambiguities – the *texture* of experience, not the substance. I remember the day I listened to Anthony Eden, defending, as I believed at the time, the values of decency and democracy, because it pulled into its orbit a hundred other less memorable days: playing war games with my brother in the family orchard; watching the parades on Anzac Day, stirred by the music and the uniforms and the sudden flash of medals; envying my classmate chosen, because her father had been killed in the war, to lay a wreath at the school memorial gates; sitting in a hushed cinema watching *Reach for the Sky*, fantasising that my father, my *real* father, was an RAF pilot killed – of course: how else to explain his absence? – in a fierce dog fight over the English Channel ... Connections. *Textures*. Patterns. Memories shaped by facts, but not defined by them. The waking dreams that make us who we are, forged in what Andrew O'Hagan described as the 'unstable border between fiction and non fiction', which is imagination's true home.

'I write fiction and I'm told it's autobiography. I write autobiography and

I'm told it's fiction,' Philip Roth famously complained in his novel, *Deception*. Recently someone close to me accused me of basing a character in one of my novels on him. 'Course it's not you,' I protested. 'He may have some of your characteristics, but he also has characteristics of ...' (and I named two other people known to us both). But that only made things worse. Explaining what goes on in the process of changing the lived life into fiction is beyond the skill of even the greatest writers. Roth's exasperated response to the criticisms levelled at him, O'Hagan's definition of the porous relationship between fact and fiction, merely highlight the problem. I should, I realise now, have answered my critic with the words I once heard Doris Lessing use in response to a similar accusation ...

I'm at a dinner party in North London in the early 70s. Lessing, while not yet elevated to the stratosphere of the Nobel Laureates, is already famous as the author of the seminal *Golden Notebook.* One of the guests, a near neighbour, accuses her jokingly of using not just his life but his cat in her latest fiction. Lessing gives him a withering look (she was good at those) and says, in the curt tones of an ill-tempered schoolmistress, 'Nonsense! I am a fiction writer. Everything I write is fiction ...'

And everything is autobiographical, as has also been said.

So, for the record, this is not an autobiography. To write that I would have to write about people dear to me, whose stories, though partly mine, are not wholly mine to tell. But it is not fiction either. Fiction has begun to fail me, or I have begun to fail it, so I have turned (by a degree or two only) to memoir. So that is what this is. I will try to stay true to the facts, avoiding invention but guided, as I cannot help but be, as I have always been, by imagination.

* * *

I'm now nineteen. A much better age. I'm not always *pretending* to be an adult. Sometimes I really am one. Like now. Hurrying along a Dunedin street to meet my boyfriend. I'm in my final year at university. We're meeting for coffee in a break between my lectures and his work as a law clerk. An assignation in a café that claims to know how to make cappuccino is a new and exciting thing to be doing in 1959, when even Nescafé is considered sophisticated. So far Dunedin can boast only two authentic coffee bars, but by the end of the year there will be more. The one I'm hurrying to is in George Street, opposite Knox Presbyterian Church. Presbyterianism is in the air you breathe in this town. It is also, and always will be, in my bloodstream.

I'm wearing a grey pleated skirt, a pale-blue cardigan buttoned at the back and a brown suede jacket, a cast-off from a friend. My wardrobe, like my life, is haphazard. I aspire to look like the girls I most admire, many of them daughters of wealthy farmers. They are part of the 'in' crowd, a world my foster sister, the one with whom – if my initial memory is correct – I listened to Anthony Eden's speech, belongs to as of right. But I have neither the means nor the artistry to achieve the necessary look. My hair, which is fine, straight and flyaway, and was till recently, on the orders of my mother, hideously permed, is covered by a gaudily patterned scarf. No one in the 'in' crowd wears headscarves. Or has badly permed hair. (My self-consciousness about my hair will last a lifetime. At one point in my early married life I removed all the mirrors from the house. I was pregnant. My hair, I was convinced, was falling out. It wasn't. It was my sanity that was failing. But I will never stop longing for hair so thick and riotously curly, birds could nest in it.)

The boyfriend I'm hurrying to meet is not my first, though the list, compared to those of most of my contemporaries, is short. Only one stands out: Paul, a cadet farmer on the South Canterbury sheep station where I worked for two summers as a cook and nanny. Paul was handsome, kind and 'well spoken'. (It will be many years before I identify this tendency of mine to fall in love with voices, but by then it's too late to avoid the traps.) Sunday after Sunday Paul tried to teach me how to water ski, succeeding only on the penultimate Sunday of my contracted stay. Paul and I weren't serious, that's the story I told when I got back to Dunedin. A summer fling, that's all it was. But the truth is that I had only to hold hands with a member of the opposite sex for alarm bells to start ringing. At eighteen – the age I was when I met Paul – everything to do with sex terrified me. I felt all the things a young healthy teenager could be expected to feel, but I could handle those feelings only by translating them into the language of love. Not that I used that language with Paul. I had enough sense to know what a mistake that would be. But I used it to myself.

Dreaming of love, turning the slightest physical contact into evidence of the longed-for state of being 'in love', was bad enough. Even worse was the urge to please, which gripped me the moment my sexual feelings were engaged. Why this should be is a mystery to me still. I loved my adoptive father but feared my mother, so shouldn't my urge to please have had women as its focus, not men? I can choose to blame the (mostly benign) patriarchy in which I was raised, not to mention the romantic films – Doris Day/Rock Hudson – pouring out of Hollywood straight into my head, but that doesn't really answer the question. All I know is that somewhere in the midst of all that pleasing I lost sight of how to please myself.

Meeting for coffee, going to the pictures, playing tennis (though with autumn fast approaching as I skip along George Street, that's about to stop), showing up at regular Saturday night parties and 'wool-store hops', ours is a conventional romance coloured by the mostly happy exigencies of student life and the powerful sense of the future which this old – by New Zealand standards – university town exudes. Both of us live in colleges, he from choice, me as a result of a court order engineered by my mother. For more than three years I was an unofficial foster child, living initially with generous and loving neighbours (in whose home I'm ninety per cent sure I listened to that Suez broadcast), then, when proximity to my mother became a problem, with the family of a school friend. Now my mother, restored to sanity after another round of shock treatment, has decreed I must live in St Margaret's College, a women's hostel. I hate it! Obliged to eat meals at the same time every day, to be locked up by 9pm (to be out till 10pm requires special permission), to follow rules that have never applied to my male counterparts in Knox and Selwyn Colleges, brings out the rebel in me. With no thought of the consequences – where would I live? how would I support myself? – I resolve to get myself expelled. I stay out all night, an offence guaranteed to lead to expulsion. Nothing happens. A few weeks later I discover from a chance remark of the matron's that she is a friend of my mother's, a member of a group of fierce, mostly single women dedicated to 'good works' whom, as a child, I christened 'the cardigan ladies'. So there's the explanation. My mother is still pulling the strings.

Just as I am resigning myself to my imprisonment, Nature intervenes. I become ill. Subject since early childhood to nose bleeds, I have one that won't stop. I'm taken to hospital from where, to my surprise and delight, I'm rescued by the mother of my university friend, Jocelyn. For the rest of this momentous year (I become engaged to my boyfriend in August), untroubled by my mother or the law, I live with a family I happily claim as my own.

By the end of the year I am a married woman.

# Chapter Three

'In any situation it is almost impossible to know what is really happening to us,' Ted Hughes wrote in his anthology, *Poetry in the Making*. 'The meaning of our experience is finally unfathomable.' So what I am feeling as I walk down the aisle of the ugly brick church of my childhood, dressed in my bridal finery, is not at all what I was expecting to feel. I'm in a state of high anxiety. Will my veil fall off? Should I have asked my brother rather than 'Uncle Charles', my foster father, to give me away? Did I make the right decisions about dresses, my own and my bridesmaids'? My young soon-to-be sisters-in-law have come to the church dressed as flower girls. Are they angry that I didn't include them in the wedding party?

But the loudest question in my head is the one concerning my mother. Her psychiatrist has assured me she won't make a fuss. The tranquillisers he has prescribed will see to that. But she has come to church dressed from head to foot in black, with a vivid, clown-like smear of lipstick across her mouth (she who has always despised people who wear make-up). What if she yells 'Jezebel!' in the middle of the service? It's happened before, though never in church. What will my new family, my two sets of in-laws – both of my fiancé's parents are divorced and re-married – think of me if that happens?

The minister officiating at the service is my cousin Tom. Years later I will learn that he, on being told of my engagement, travelled to Wellington to seek information about my birth parents. Too many people had remarked how alike my fiancé and I were. The fact that my prospective father-in-law had attended Otago University at a time that made it theoretically possible for him to be my father had not escaped my beady-eyed cousin. I don't know what Tom discovered in Wellington, but it was not the identity of my father. His name was not on the birth certificate. Was Tom shocked to discover that this was the norm, that only the mother's name is recorded for all to see? Was he further shocked to discover that illegitimate births were registered separately from legitimate ones? I will never know. But he must have found out enough to be satisfied that my marriage would not be incestuous, because here he is, in his Presbyterian robe and dog collar, grinning at me as I speak the words that will turn me into a wife. 'For better for worse, for richer for poorer ... till death do us part.'

* * *

Dreams of the future. Like all twenty-year-olds, my head is full of them. I'm barely out of my teens, but I long for a child. I'm living a married life in a lakeside house belonging to my mother-in-law, but the place I want to be, where it's been agreed we'll go when we've saved enough money, is England. I have a job with the New Zealand Broadcasting Service (NZBS) in Rotorua, but the life I imagine, waking and sleeping, has the shape and sound and smell of the theatre. As I adjust to answering to a new surname, I metamorphose from Elspeth to Susan. (No one in my new life calls me 'Nook', the nickname my father gave me, the one name that to this day spells home.) Till recently I believed this new Christian name was given to me by my young sisters-in-law, Elspeth being too much of a mouthful, but they have assured me they had nothing to do with it. So the question of who bestowed the name on me, and why, remains unanswered. As does the question of why I agreed to it ...

Meantime, I go about my daily business with my head full of Stanislavsky's advice to actors – I read his entire oeuvre while working on the Canterbury sheep station – and whole scenes from Shakespeare, memorised during my years as a passionate member of the Dunedin Shakespeare Society. Lines from Chekov, Ibsen and the Greeks vie for supremacy in my busy, secret mind with lines from a new play from Australia – *Summer of the Seventeenth Doll* – which I have now read four times. I could have been an actor. That's what I tell myself. Thanks to my drama teacher at school, I was given the chance to apply for a scholarship to the Bristol Old Vic Drama School. That I didn't pursue it is down to cowardice – how would I live? where would I live? would I make any friends? – and my abiding fear of giving offence. No one, apart from me and my drama teacher, thought I should be an actor. A dubious profession, at best, in the minds of most of the people in my life. 'Do a degree first. Get something solid under your belt. Then see ...'

Now that I'm a married woman it's assumed all that theatrical nonsense has been forgotten.

Working for the NZBS is not my first full-time job. There were the two consecutive summers working as a cook and nanny; two earlier summers working on a Central Otago orchard; a disastrous summer picking raspberries in Nelson. (It rained, the crop was ruined, I made almost no money.) Since the death of my father the only money in my pocket has been the money I've earned. My mother controlled the purse strings as she controlled, till I married, much of my life. The miracle is that she ever gave permission for me to marry. I suspect the fact that my future father-in-law was a respected gynaecologist had something to do with it. My mother had been a nurse. Doctors, in her world view, were the nearest thing to gods walking on Earth.

My job title is Transcription Officer. The work – packing up tapes hired from the BBC or on loan from various radio stations around the country, then ferrying them to the post office – is dull and repetitive, and would have driven me crazy were it not for the company of my fellow workers. Their persistent chatter may interrupt my day-dreaming, but I am happy to be part of their team. By the end of my first week they have come up with a ribald alternative to my married name, adding yet another moniker to my list. Not that I mind. I'm as comfortable with invented names as I am with invented histories. So I tell my new friends I'm not really a New Zealander, I'm an Australian. My father was killed in the war, my mother died of a broken heart. It never occurs to me that I could be caught out telling these elaborate fairy tales. I need them, therefore they are true.

Morning and afternoon tea are the high points of my working day. The weeks are signed off with Friday night fish and chips at the home of the closest of my new friends. Gradually I become used to the pervasive Rotorua smell. After weekends away, visiting my in-laws in Auckland, I am always glad to return to the sulphurous town and the daily ritual of driving to work from the house on Lake Okareka. It may not feel like home, but I love the sound of the frogs at night, and the looming presence of Mount Tarawera across the water. And I love the drive over bush-covered hills, past lakes that seem to have been coloured by a mad impressionist painter. I don't find the filmy grey waters of Lake Rotorua or the sleepy town built on its shores beautiful, but I'm grateful for the temporary haven this corner of New Zealand has provided. Rotorua was never going to be more than a stepping stone. Soon my body will follow my head and heart to England. That is the plan. Not a trip, not the customary OE, but the beginning of a new life.

Shortly after I start work, I join the local repertory society, affectionately known as The Shambles. I play the lead in a French farce, take a smaller role in an Agatha Christie mystery (my husband plays the judge), then play another lead in Enid Bagnold's *The Chalk Garden*. At last my passionate love of theatre has found a place to express itself. But there are undercurrents. Theatre, particularly the amateur kind, can act as a magnet for unhappy souls. I wouldn't have described myself as unhappy in those first months of married life, more that I was suffering from a mysterious malaise, but I can't deny the connection I felt with others, women and men, whose dissatisfaction was expressed in a dozen unstated ways. Intrigue was in the air. So was sex. I can't now remember who was supposed to be sleeping with whom, or what was fact and what was rumour, only that there was a strong whiff of seduction in the energy generated at rehearsals.

A year and a half later, I leave Rotorua. As I stand on the shores of Lake Okareka watching the swans glide in and out of the reeds, dancing, so I have persuaded myself, to appease the angry god of the mountain across the water, I am certain I'm saying goodbye forever. But by the end of the decade, in circumstances I could never have imagined, I will be back.

**Return to Rotorua**

I'm looking for a girl I knew twenty plus years ago, a
girl like any other.
She'd look at men and say, I'll marry him, or
he'd give me a jolly life.

She'd look at kids and say, I'd call her Sam,
short for Samantha, and him
Richard, never Dick.

She'd look at houses,
see tables bright with candlelight,
plan intimate dinners for couples from the same walk of life.

I've looked by the lake where she lived,
peered through the window of the room in which she slept,
climbed hills she climbed,
walked streets whose names, like other members of her tribe, she
mispronounced ...

Distant voices hum inside my head.
If I can't find her, she must be dead.

# Chapter Four

June 1962. I'm standing on the deck of the *Fairsea*, a converted Italian aircraft carrier. As the streamers linking us to family and friends snap and rise gracefully into the air, I tell myself, This is it, The First Day of the Rest of My Life. Others might weep, but I am dry-eyed. Plans have been made; money saved. Now we're on our way. I don't even want to watch the land of my birth disappear over the horizon. I prefer to stare at the sea frothing around the edges of the ship, swirling in a white-tipped frenzy all the way to the horizon.

'The *Fairsea* at first acquaintance looked quite glamorous, painted white, it seemed a trim, streamlined ship that one could imagine gliding gracefully over the blue waters.' I can hardly believe I wrote that shamefully clichéd sentence, but I did, just as I wrote these equally dull words a few days later: 'The entrance to Brisbane is by river, an interesting journey which takes a considerable time.'

Discovering I had kept a journal of not just the sea voyage, but the year and a half that followed – as it turned out, this *was* just a trip, not the Beginning of Everything that I had imagined – came as a shock. Till that moment I would have said I'd never kept a diary. Thoughts, quotes, observations, those I *have* kept, scribbled haphazardly in notebooks with no reference or filing system to make sense of them. Many's the hour I've wasted searching for something I dimly remember writing down. But here in front of me is the evidence: a diary, discovered while searching through letters and photos for my earlier memoir, *What Lies Beneath*. Indeed, I kept two, though I prefer to think of them as journals, since while I accept the truth of the facts recorded on those neat, lined pages, I do not recognise the 'voice' of the author. Did someone give me the hard-backed exercise book which I filled first with an almost daily record of the voyage on the *Fairsea*, then with a record, abruptly broken off, of our time in England? The last entry, written in Brighton where we'd gone for a searingly hot, unforgettably vivid Whitsun weekend, reads, 'I will stop now and take an afternoon nap.' Why did I stop? And since when did I take afternoon naps? Is the answer to both questions to be found in the disconnect between what was going on in my head – the fairy tales I told myself and others – and the daily realities of my life? Or was it that I decided keeping a journal (like writing a memoir?) was a sign of self-absorption, and best put a stop to by 'taking a nap'?

The journals are beside me now, the writing careful and legible (something that cannot be said of my later handwriting), the content as harmless as a Sunday sermon. Reading them I can find no trace of the writer I was to become. No wonder my first attempts at fiction were so ham-fisted. Words, it seemed, back then, scared me as much as the thought of giving offence. I scribbled all the time, on the back of my hand, in letters home, in those pesky, mostly lost notebooks, but the words didn't set me free. Only as a reader, or on those blissful occasions when I had work as an actor, did I find release.

But a diary, even a dull and dutiful one, *is* an aide-memoire, so at least I know what I'm writing here is fact, not the 'biographical mud' of memory. Though I have to admit, as I plough my way through the lists of people met and places visited, I have the same reaction as when I'm sent one of those Christmas missives that detail the doings of the sender and his/her family over the last year. I want to shout, 'Don't tell me what you did, tell me what you *feel*!'

Early on in the voyage I fall ill with scarlet fever. Five people die. It's assumed the cause of death is the same fever that has confined me to our pocket-handkerchief cabin (so small only one person can get dressed at a time), but in the absence of any official information all anyone can do is speculate. The bodies of the five dead passengers are thrown over the rails at dawn. In my feverish state I start to believe the ship is doomed. As it turns out I'm not wrong. Its very next voyage will be its last. Somewhere in the Mediterranean, the *Fairsea* catches fire. No one dies, but the ship is a write-off, and the captain, the same man who steered us across the oceans of the world, commits suicide.

* * *

Patterns. Fiction writers look for them everywhere. Recently I was a guest at the Going West Festival in Titirangi, Auckland. One of the sessions concerned the house I'd lived in during the 1990s when I was married to the writer Maurice Shadbolt. I'd decided not to attend – my memories of that house, and those years, are complex to say the least – but at the last minute, persuaded by the friends I was staying with, I changed my mind. Various things not germane to this narrative happened during that hour-long session. More than once tears threatened. Then a casual remark, of no interest to anyone but me, pricked the bubble of memory into which I had retreated, and blew it away.

In 1963, after a period living in England, Maurice and his first wife, Gill, travelled back to New Zealand on the *Castel Felice*, sister ship to the *Fairsea*, which had taken me to England the year before. Not a momentous coincidence – Thomas Hardy wouldn't have given it the time of day – but one that nonetheless stopped me in my tracks. Perhaps I should call it a trigger rather than a coincidence, but it still leaves intact the image that formed in my mind the moment I heard the words *Castel Felice*. Sister ships passing on the high seas ... Either everything is significant, or nothing is. And since I long ago chose to believe the former and not the latter, I see a pattern in my picture of passing ships, heralding a future I could never have imagined but have since lived.

The present, Julian Barnes claims in his novel *Staring at the Sun*, is nothing but 'a pinprick between an invented past and an imagined future'. If I understand him correctly, he's saying that whatever is happening in the present moment is so composed of both a past we have invented and a future we are imagining, the effect on us is no more than a pinprick. But isn't inhabiting the present as fully as we can supposed to be the secret of happiness? The only effective response to life's existential problems, so the current mantra goes, is to be *mindful*, to bring your mind fully into the moment.

So what did happen in that unsettling session at the Going West Festival? It wasn't a pinprick I felt, more like a slap across the face. Photos were put up on the screen. A video was played. And there was Maurice, sitting in the chair he always sat in, wearing his familiar blue jersey, talking as if he and I were still married, still lovers, still living in his bush-choked house. In those few unspectacular minutes the past was laid out before me – both the past that really happened and the past I had invented. And I saw, in a flash, what Barnes meant. It's as if we have two lives, past and future, running parallel to the one we are actually living. For some hours after this *pinprick* I was not just physically disorientated, I was emotionally adrift.

I returned to this memoir sobered by the thought that what is really going on here is interrogation. There are no more journals to interrogate, only memory. But buried in that elusive organ of identity is the truth I am seeking – the why of events, the extent of my culpability, the difficulty of really knowing another person, the necessity of forgiveness.

* * *

Back on the *Fairsea* I start ticking off the ports – Brisbane, Singapore (but I'm in quarantine and not allowed off the ship), Colombo, Aden, Cairo, Naples ... Colombo, where the president has just been assassinated, sparks my nascent political interest. (Romantic Toryism, which has yielded to my husband's far more rigorous socialism, has been cheerfully tossed overboard.) Listening to accounts of what is going on in Ceylon, as it was called at the time, I become painfully aware of my ignorance. Reaching the Suez Canal, shocked by the in-your-face presence of British soldiers, I join in the chorus of contempt for Anthony Eden and his quasi-imperial adventure.

Long before we reach the equator our fellow travellers have stopped being passengers and become people with names. Geert and Elke (not their real names), a Dutch couple returning to visit their parents in Rotterdam, shock me with their criticisms of New Zealand. I may not want to live in the land of my birth, but I'm not comfortable when people who are not Kiwis describe it as 'dull' and 'backward'. Geert tells me he's decided against taking up citizenship, not because the country is dull and backward, but because it costs five pounds to become a citizen. Others – French, Australian, Polish, British – spice up my days with their stories, conjuring up images of lives as different from mine as the ones I still, from time to time, shamefully, invent.

Two people stand out. Jill is English, Tony Australian. She is a top London model; he is a playwright, son of the conductor of the Sydney Symphony Orchestra. They are newly married and dazzlingly glamorous. Having tried, following their London wedding, to live in Australia (another 'dull and backward' country, apparently) they are on their way 'home' to England. I watch Jill flirting with the captain – a sleekly handsome Italian, unaware of the tragedy awaiting him – her elegant, androgynous body barely clothed as we near the tropics. I feel fat and frumpy alongside her. Tony is both proud of his wife's ability to attract men and worried by it. The four of us become friends. We drink cocktails together before dinner, and play, reluctantly at first, then with growing enthusiasm, after-dinner games of cards and Scrabble.

* * *

Cairo. A city I will return to, in very different circumstances, a decade and a half later, researching for my novel *Love and War*. A city that will come to stand in my mind for the extremes of human behaviour: cruelty co-existing with kindness; chaos doing its best to choke any semblance of order. I meet, on that later visit, a young medical student who wants to walk with me to practise his English. We become friends. I visit his family, who treat me like an honoured guest. I am in this ancient capital to trace the movements of New Zealand soldiers stationed here during World War II, but what I take away with me, what will outlast the scribbled notes, roughly drawn maps and poorly focused photographs, are images of a place so completely 'other' it would have seemed, had it not been for the kindness of my medical friend and his family, to belong in an alien universe. The sights – blue-ceilinged mosques, men in white galabiya, black-robed women, the mighty Nile splintering the city, a red-rimmed sun hanging out of the sky like a diseased eye; the smells – dirt, dust, diesel, spices, sweet oranges, sweat; the sounds – shouting, tooting, chanting, whistles blowing, calls to prayer from the city's many minarets – these are the things I will never forget.

But on that first visit, in 1962, I felt only hot confusion and a desire to be back in the manacled safety of our cabin. We are in the bazaar. Jill and Tony, seasoned travellers, are our guides. Stall holders on all sides are trying to separate us from our money. A man approaches us, not a stall holder, a 'gentleman' dressed in European clothes. He asks my husband, in halting English, if I'm his sister. Hysteria threatens. This place is too much! Many people have commented on my likeness to my husband, but no one has gone so far as to ask if we're brother and sister. Then I realise something else is going on. The man wants to buy me. My husband, his sense of humour rising to the challenge, starts to bargain. It's all crazily surreal, and of course makes a wonderful story to tell people, but I can't help wondering what would have happened if a bargain had been struck. Would the man have called on the law to defend him, demanding, like Shylock, that he be given his 'pound of flesh'?

* * *

Finally we reach England, home of Shakespeare and Dickens, Hardy and Thackeray, Lawrence and George Eliot (to whom, decades later, I will discover I am distantly related through my birth family, a fact I seize on with delight, creating a pattern where doubtless none exists). The journal records the day as wet and cold. The date is August the 10th, the height of summer.

# Chapter Five

The England of 1962 is a land still wearing the visible scars of war, still paying lip service to the mores of a broken social order. Away from the tired green of the countryside (this is August: the leaves are browning at the edges; the fields are stripped of their harvest), the predominant colour is grey: grey skies; grey faces; shabby grey buildings, many still bearing witness to the Luftwaffe's firepower. What I can't know as we wend our way by bus from Southampton to London is that this world is about to be transformed. By the end of the decade it will be a world of Technicolor, of social and sexual revolution, of the Beatles and Monty Python, and 'winds of change' blowing not just through Africa but around the entire globe.

We are to stay at the Overseas Visitors Club in Earls Court. How this came about I've no idea, but I suspect my in-laws had something to do with it. My journal records, in Pooterish detail, both the arrival at the club (I eat steak, I wash my hair, we sleep in a double bed), and our initially fruitless hunt for a flat. I complain about the high rents (seven pounds fifty a week!) and the terrible hygiene. I comment on the voices I hear in the streets. Earls Court is not just home to colonials – Kiwis, Aussies, Canadians, South Africans, Jamaicans, Rhodesians – it's a magnet for refugees from the ruins of war in Europe. I describe my first sight of Trafalgar Square and Nelson's Column as 'exciting'; my first visit to a

West End show – Peter Schaffer's *The Private Ear and the Public Eye* (a play I would act in myself five years later) starring Maggie Smith – as 'thrilling'. I don't recognise the writer of this dreary travelogue. Where is the person who, on her first walk from Oxford Circus down Regent Street to Piccadilly Circus, felt she was levitating, sensing in every street name, every statue, every ancient public building and church a connection that went deeper than her reading about these places and the people who walked these streets? Where is the record of those friendly ghosts who accompanied her on these walks, their fingers circling her elbow as they guided her through the Promised Land?

'Travelled to the West End by tube' is how I start the description of my first day in London. 'Very quick and efficient but rather mechanised and impersonal. People travelling on the tube seem to share the same expression – dispirited and generally fed-up.' (Years later my first publisher will deplore my use of words like 'seem' and 'quite' and 'rather'. 'Too many qualifying words,' he will complain. 'Too many adverbs.' I could say the same to the writer of the inoffensive journal now open in front of me.)

Five days after our arrival in London we sign the lease on a flat in Redcliffe Gardens (actually 'flat' is too grand, it's a bed-sitter). We persuade ourselves we can afford the seven pounds ten shillings a week rent and will survive the primitive plumbing arrangements. The water in the shared loo on the landing is the colour of weak tea. The smell is indescribable. But the bed-sit, though dark and displaying mysterious stains on carpets and walls, has all the necessary furniture, and is large enough for the bed to be disguised as an extra sofa. Besides, it looks out over a garden, neglected but with welcome patches of green. What I don't yet know is that the windows don't fit, so that when the November fogs arrive I will be forced to stuff the gaps with newspaper to prevent being overcome by choking fumes. This will be one of London's worst smogs. (The dictionary defines smog as 'fog intensified by smoke or other atmospheric pollutants'.) It will also, thanks to an Act of Parliament, be one of its last.

In 2014 I visit my New Zealand nephew in the home he shares with his partner just around the corner from Redcliffe Gardens. The contrast between the way my nephew lives now and the way we lived then could not be greater. The façades may look the same, but that is all. My nephew's flat is all light and colour and shiny surfaces, with french doors opening onto a stunning miniature garden. But I like it that he lives so close to my old home. The coincidence of it may not be powerful enough to create a pattern, but it feeds the appetite that *wants* there to be a pattern. And when I step out onto the street again there are still foreign voices, and double-decker buses, and weary commuters shuffling out of the underground.

I set about turning the Redcliffe Gardens bed-sit into a home. I pick up cheap off-cuts and use them to disguise the stains on the sofa and chairs. I hand sew (very badly) bright, greeny-blue curtains. I buy prints – a Utrillo, a Van Gogh, a Paris poster – and hang them where they will best disguise the water marks on the wallpaper. A decade later, living permanently in England, I will cover my walls with New Zealand prints and paintings, but in 1962 I don't even want to remember New Zealand. Home is a large, crudely furnished room, a kitchen the size of a cupboard hidden behind a bead curtain, a Zip water heater that either scalds your hand or doesn't heat the water at all, the aforementioned loo, and a bath, tucked behind a screen, that must have once been white but is now, like some strange, miscegenated animal, covered with spots and stripes in varying shades of yellow and brown.

Ten days later, as the proud owners not just of a London address but of a car – a second-hand minivan in which we plan to sleep – we set off on a tour of southern England, a holiday before the reality of the need to work takes over. On our second to last day we drive to Cambridge, where Margot and Angus, who rescued me from St Margaret's, are spending a sabbatical. I remember, as clearly as if it were yesterday, Angus telling me about his conversations with E.M. Forster, who was at the time an honorary fellow of King's College, but there's no mention of this in the journal. I had by then read all of Forster's novels except *Maurice*, which wouldn't be published till after his death. I consider him one of the greatest English novelists. To be a mere two degrees of separation from him must have been thrilling. So why the silence?

Angus and Margot take us to evensong at King's College (might Forster have been there?); to tea at Rupert Brooke's Grantchester; to the Cambridge Arts Theatre to see *Domino*, a French comedy; to the cathedrals of Ely and Peterborough; to Wisbech in search of a Jesuit concentration camp from the time of Elizabeth I (a quest of Angus the historian). I describe these outings in my journal as variously 'impressive' (the cathedrals), 'harmonious' (Grantchester), 'delightful' (the Cambridge Arts Theatre) and 'sublime' (evensong). Reading these lines I find myself thinking of Ingrid Bergman (knowing she'd had a child out of wedlock, I used to fantasise that she was my mother) who, when asked in an interview how she felt as an older woman looking at a film of her younger self, answered that she recognised the young woman, and acknowledged responsibility for her, but she didn't really know her. I feel the same way about the person who wrote this dispiriting journal.

We return to London, to the chilly signs of autumn and the pressing need to earn money. Suddenly I am in a world I know nothing about. I want to be an actor. How on earth do I make that happen? I know no one in the profession. I've not been to any of the recognised drama schools. I prepare a CV so short it makes me feel like an imposter. I look up dramatic agencies in the phone book. I choose the one with the largest advertisement and, miraculously, I'm invited in for an interview. Three days later I'm walking down The Strand repeating the words, 'I'm an actress. I have an agent', over and over in my head.

My first job is to play a suburban housewife in a television ad. This is followed, after a gap, by a small part in a children's show, filmed live. But then the work dries up. 'You need better photos,' my agent tells me. 'The ones you've given me don't do you justice.' So I spend, guiltily, what seems like a vast sum of money getting the right kind of photos taken. Seeing myself in *Spotlight*, the magazine that showcases actors for hire, gives me a queasy feeling. I don't recognise myself in the photographs, or in the words my agent has written about me. Is this because I sensed even then that marriage and the theatre are a difficult mix? Or was I once again too frightened to take the next step?

I follow this nervous, self-conscious young woman as, with shoulders slumped and fingers spelling out words on the back of her hand, she creeps to and from auditions, and I want to give her a good hard shake. The words I would have her spell out are not the random offerings on the back of her hand, they are Nelson Mandela's, from his 1994 inaugural speech: 'Our deepest fear is not that we are inadequate. Our deepest fear is that we are powerful beyond measure. It is our light, not our darkness, that most frightens us …' But I suspect she wouldn't have listened.

After several weeks of sitting around waiting for the phone to ring – the reality of the jobbing actor's life – I take a 'proper' job, in a coffee bar near the Earls Court tube station, a short walk from Redcliffe Gardens. The Corillo – it means 'meeting place' in Spanish – has pretensions, but is in fact a dump. First thing I notice about it is the smell – stale cigarette smoke and something else I can't identify. I'm taken to the staff quarters in the basement, where the smell intensifies. I see a cockroach scuttling across the floor, then another. Do cockroaches smell? I'm put on dishwashing duty. During the course of the day I meet the rest of the staff, a regular United Nations of cooks and waitresses, coffee makers and helping hands: Lucas from Bombay, José from Barcelona, Edmundo from Turin, Aristo from Athens, Jennifer from Dublin, Sissy from Oslo, Cristine from Hamburg, Eduardo from Madrid. Peggy, the manager, is Cockney. She has names – none of them complimentary – for every member of staff. Mr Fuelling, the owner, she calls Sleaze. When, after three months, I hand in my notice, I tell Sleaze the wages he pays are a disgrace. (I have never accepted the argument in favour of tipping: Sleaze was making a fortune out of our sweated labour. Besides, who tips the poor 'helping hand' washing dishes?) 'You'd never get away with it in New Zealand,' I add piously, as my indignant ex-boss shows me the door.

* * *

With my wages from The Corillo we acquire a television set. I watch the prime minister, Harold Macmillan, make speeches on the Common Market, which

Britain has applied to join; listen, on the radio, to a re-run of his speech to the parliament of South Africa about the 'winds of change' blowing across the continent. I'm in favour of independence for Britain's former colonies (though I feel a twinge of sadness watching, on TV, the Union Jack come down), but I am not in favour of the Common Market. Despite my conversion to socialism, there is still a bit of the Romantic Tory in me. I want Britain to head a powerful Commonwealth, not become part of a United States of Europe. Had I known then what I know now about British rule in Kenya and elsewhere, I would have felt differently. But in 1962 I still believed in the Good Englishman and his right to rule if not *the* world, then at least *his* world, which happened at the time also to be mine.

As I write this, Britain is about to vote on whether to stay in the EU, as it is now called. How would I vote if I was living there still? Probably, reluctantly, to stay in, since I have nothing in common with UKIP and the Little Englandism that is driving the Brexit movement. But I reserve the right to be suspicious of large trading deals, especially in this age of global capitalism. Free trade sounds like something we should all want until you ask the question, who is it free for? With the gap between rich and poor widening every year, I don't see much evidence of free trade helping the growing numbers of low-wage earners, unemployed, refugees and disabled, whose plight many (though not all) of the governments of the 'Free World' seem able, with very little sign of conscience, to ignore.

'Selling the family silver' was the phrase Harold Macmillan used in the 1980s to describe the enthusiasm of a very different Tory prime minister – Margaret Thatcher – for selling off British assets to the highest bidder. Telecommunications, public transport, water, gas and electricity were all traded for the cash Thatcher needed to push through her tax reforms, shifting the burden of taxation from the 'wealth creators' to the wage-earning class. A new world order was emerging, one in which not just trade, but markets, would be free. 'History,' the economist and philosopher Francis Fukuyama famously declared, 'is dead.' But he was wrong. Western-style democracy did not take over the world, as he had predicted. And those who believed him, who refused to heed the lessons of history, led us, in the decades that followed the selling of the family silver, into wars that seem, now, to have no end in sight.

There wasn't a great deal of difference between the world lived in by the teenager who listened to Anthony Eden on the radio and that of the young woman who watched Macmillan's speech on television, but change was coming. Four decades later we live in a world neither of my young selves would have recognised. Is it a better world? History will be the judge.

# Chapter Six

Some months after our arrival in England we meet two people whose lives will intersect with mine in profound ways. I don't remember how we met them, though I suspect they came into our orbit through the 'Kiwi mafia', of which we are inevitably a part. Most of the people who come to our bed-sit for meals or somewhere to 'camp' are Kiwis. Most are known to us, but some aren't. Someone 'back home' has given them our address.

John and Shirley are Kiwis who left New Zealand in the wake of World War II. Both were (no longer are when I meet them) Quakers. John, a convinced pacifist, was arrested at the age of twenty-one and held in a prison for violent offenders in the central North Island. I'm not sure how much of this I learn at that first meeting, but once I have the story whole in my mind I'm forced to look at my own country through an altogether darker lens. The worst I could have said about it till then was that it lacked excitement. Now I begin to see that the problems associated with isolation and a small population are only the surface of things. What lay beneath that bland appearance was an insistence on conformity that could turn sinister.

John is a producer at the BBC. Shirley teaches classics at a girls' grammar school. It doesn't take long for me to see that these are people for whom no subject is off limits. We talk about homosexual law reform, the role of the unions in the Labour Party, the problem of Ireland and the IRA, the existence (or not) of God, state education, constitutional monarchy, the class system, the meaning of family … debating everything as if our own futures, and the future of the world beyond our doors, depends on it.

With John in mind I read about New Zealand's treatment of pacifists in both world wars, and the seed of the novel I will write a decade and a half later is sown. *Love and War*, dedicated to John and Shirley, will attract interest from three different film companies, earning me more than I've earned for any other novel before or since.

The first time I visit their home – it's in High Barnett, a long tube ride from central London – I am filled with the sense of something good starting. I may have left my homeland behind, but I'm drawn to my fellow Kiwis like a moth to light. I'm particularly drawn to those who describe themselves, as I've secretly begun to do, as expatriates. We eat a typical Kiwi meal – meat and three veg – sitting around the table with John and Shirley's impressively well-behaved children. All four, encouraged by their school-teaching mother and brilliant father, will go to Oxford. If there was pressure to perform well academically I didn't feel it, either on that first night or subsequently. But later, when I am living a very different life in the Cotswolds, their younger son will abscond from Oxford, disappearing without trace for over a year. By this time my life is so entwined with theirs I feel their anguish as if it were my own. John takes leave of absence from the BBC to sit for hours every day in the bank his son used, hoping he will show up (he never did: his account remained untouched). When he and Shirley, and sometimes their other children, come to my home in the Cotswolds for weekends, we wear ourselves out on long walks, trying desperately to talk of anything but the absent son and brother. At the end of that year we all spend Christmas together in John and Shirley's Dorset cottage, visiting houses open to the public so that Shirley can indulge her passion (shared by one of her sons) for landscaped gardens. On one unforgettable occasion John and I opt out of the garden tour, choosing instead to sit in his car and talk. John, his anguish visible now that Shirley is not there to see it, questions himself remorselessly.

Was there something he did, or failed to do, that triggered his son's decision to bolt? Suddenly he is back at the start of it all, to the day he and Shirley met: a Labour Party rally in Auckland, both of them barely twenty. Shirley fell for him right away. He took longer. Later, when he was in prison near Ruapehu, Shirley visited him (a difficult feat in wartime New Zealand) as often as the law allowed. By the time he was released it was more or less assumed they would marry. But he was quick to reassure me he loved her. Perhaps not as she loved him, but he was always glad to come home to her.

His story ends, and he turns to me. 'Do you think ...?' he begins. But he doesn't finish the sentence.

'Aren't most marriages a bit unequal?' I suggest, after we've sat in silence for a few moments. I've had to guess where that sentence was headed, but when I see the look on his face I know my intuition was correct. 'There's a saying, isn't there?' I go on. 'Something about there being one who kisses and one who is kissed. The lover and the loved. It doesn't mean something's wrong. Wherever he is your son knows you love him, you and Shirley both. That's what will matter to him. What will always matter to him. The equality of that shared love.'

Looking back now, I can see John and I were probably a little in love with each other. But nothing was ever said. Did Shirley sense this? Is that why, when I visited her in the early 1990s, she suddenly attacked not just me but the novel I had dedicated to her and John? Till recently I would have said that was a question I couldn't answer, but a chance contact in Auckland with a friend of the family has provided an explanation of sorts. John's final illness happened after I'd moved back to New Zealand. What the friend told me filled me with sadness. 'He wanted to die on his own terms,' he explained, 'but Shirley couldn't let that happen. She had to be in charge. So he turned away from her ...'

The missing son eventually returned and was reintegrated into the family. No explanation was asked for, nor, so far as I know, given. I miss John. And I miss his bright, questing children. As for my relationship with Shirley, I think of it now as a 'spent friendship', a phrase I first heard in conversation with the New Zealand writer Eric McCormick. 'When friendships run their course, you have no choice but to accept it and move on,' he said. Eric didn't know Shirley, so it wasn't her we were talking about. But I took his words to heart, and was comforted.

* * *

After I give up my job at The Corillo I go to work as a glorified babysitter for a family in Maida Vale. It's mostly evening work, which leaves me free to go to auditions, but from time to time I'm summoned to look after the two 'babies', Jeremy and Amanda, during the day. My journal entries for this time seem to have been written by a zombie. 'Mr and Mrs Patterson have a nice flat. The central heating is always welcome after a cold journey. Amanda (three and a half) can be difficult, but she's an interesting child, and no doubt it's good for me to see the less attractive side of being with children ...'

At the end of October we set off in our minivan for a brief tour of Scotland where we both have clan connections. Too poor to sleep in guest houses, we make do with sleeping bags in the back of the van, cooking up meals on a gas cooker, splashing out only once for a decent dinner, bed and bath (the bath costs extra). We beetle our way north, bypassing, after a brief look-see, the bleak industrial cities of Sheffield and Nottingham. (A decade later I will live for six months in Nottingham and grow to love its coal-black buildings, ornate iron bridges and shadowy parks.) We spend our first night camped on the Yorkshire moors. Then it's the Lake District which, to my acute disappointment, hardly merits a mention in the journal. Windermere is dismissed as 'delightful'. Wordsworth's cottage at Grasmere is 'very pretty and quaint'. Learning, four decades later, that my birth mother's family on her father's side came from Cumbria gives the lie to my supposed ability to sense when a place has significance for me. 'Spent the night on the slopes of Skiddaw after an energetic climb to the top ...' But I should know by now that the journal wouldn't tell me even if I *had* felt a connection.

We cross into Scotland at Gretna Green and head for Kirkcudbright, where we have an address for a relative of my husband's. 'Life is very raw in these parts,' the journal pontificates. 'Only Bingo to provide entertainment, and no decent sunshine for the last three years' – information kindly provided by the barmaid at Stranraer, who boasted that she hadn't taken her cardy off since the war. On our return to London we make a pilgrimage to Tower Hill to see the memorial to Lord Lovatt, the most famous of my husband's clansmen and the last man to be beheaded in England.

'There are moments when history and memory seem like a mist, as if what really happened matters less than what should have happened,' novelist Karen Joy Fowler wrote in *We Are All Completely Beside Ourselves*. As I relive this time in my life, I can't help but ask myself if she's right. What I didn't know then, but do now, was that for me happiness is inextricably tied up with feelings of safety. I felt safe in England. Had we stayed there, far from the influences that would pull us apart, our marriage would have been tested – the sexual revolution was stirring; my need to act (later to write) was gnawing at my insides – but it would, I believe, have survived. And that is the story I *want* to write. A fiction, but one that was true, for a time.

# Chapter Seven

Money! Till this time I'd not thought of it as separate from everything else in our lives. We worked, we paid our bills, we saved for holidays. Now suddenly here it was, looming over us like an angry parent. It was my fault. So far I'd landed only three small acting jobs, each of which, being in television, paid well, but when would the next role come along? As for my work for the Pattersons, that was even more financially uncertain than acting.

So, with a heavy heart, I accept the decision to look for somewhere cheaper to live. In the same spirit I tell the Pattersons I can no longer work for them during the day, and take a job as a sales demonstrator, for which I am about as equipped as a fish to ride a bicycle. My employer – Mr Johns – I describe in the journal as a 'strange' fellow, but the more accurate adjective would be 'dodgy'. The product I am demonstrating – a non-electric floor polisher – is not just flimsy (I give it a six-month life span), it doesn't work properly. Which, as I recite my spiel to an audience largely made up of women who look as if they haven't got sixpence to spend, let alone what this doomed contraption costs, makes me feel wretched. But the money is good, so I stick it out for six weeks, travelling to stores in the less fashionable parts of London, before conscience gets the better of me and I walk off the job.

By this time we are living in Crouch Hall Road in Hornsey. Instead of the seven pounds ten shillings a week we paid in Earls Court, we are now paying three pounds three shillings. Our landlord is Conrad Russell, son of the famous earl. To our surprise – our previous landlady was cold to the point of rudeness – Conrad, whose shy friendliness I find endearing, is happy to sit and talk. But however much I like him and appreciate his keeping the rent so low, I can't conjure up much enthusiasm for our new home. Like Earls Court it's a bed-sit, but there the comparison ends. I can cheer up the interior, but I can't do much about the view from the window – rows of back yards with pint-sized sheds and rusty swings – or the genteel squalor that hits me every time I step outside the door. We move in winter, with snow lying on the ground. Our first encounter with our new neighbours is an argument over parking. The house was built in the late nineteenth century as a single dwelling, but is now divided into three flats. We've parked in a cleared space outside. An hour later there's an angry knocking on our door. The man in the flat below demands that we move our minivan immediately. *He* cleared that space, so it belongs to him. 'If you want to park in the street, clear your own bloody space!'

It's a fitting introduction to life in the underbelly of Hampstead. The Heath, and the village that shares its name, are only a fifteen-minute walk away, but Crouch Hall Road (now a highly sought-after address) belongs in a different universe. It's not just the man and his silently assenting wife in the flat below whom we manage to offend, but the elderly lady in the flat above who complains if we have the television on after 9pm, even though we routinely turn the sound down to a whisper; it's the sombrely dressed women I queue with at the butcher's, who glare at me when I ask for a leg of lamb – an uncle has sent us a frozen sheep for Christmas – while they put in their order for a shilling's worth of mince; it's the shifty-eyed men in shabby overcoats, and the women hiding their hair and their curlers under knotted headscarves, whom I encounter at the launderette. I stick out. I'm too healthy. Too privileged. These people have endured bombing, rationing and everything in between. How is it fair that I have more? That my clothes, and the food I eat, are so much better?

'It's incredible how lonely it is in this part of London,' the journal records. 'I think it's because it's so grey and depressing. The only colour is provided by huge advertisement hoardings that serve to remind you what a materialistic society this is ...' Oh dear.

Having turned my back on demonstrating faulty gadgets, and with no acting work in sight (though the BBC, for whom I have done a 'general audition', have told me I am now on their books), I sign up to do supply teaching. Apart from an occasional stint teaching piano when I was a student, I have never worked as a teacher. But no one seems bothered by my lack of training and experience. It's enough that I have a degree. Had I known what the next five months were going to be like, I would have run a mile.

On my first day I'm sent to Clemence Cave Secondary Modern School in Hornsey. I'm to take a class in geography, about which I know nothing (my degree is in English, history and French). That day will set the pattern for what follows. I don't teach, I strive, in a state of near terror, to keep order. The journal, jolted into life by the daily experience of 'What is wrong with British education', at last starts to record not just events but the feelings they generate. The word 'fear' occurs in almost every paragraph. 'I had to fight my fear every day, no doubt quite unjustified.' (Why did I say that? On one occasion I had to run from a teenage boy wielding a knife. On another, a gang of girls waylaid me on my way home, hoping to get a rise out of me with their sexually explicit taunts.) I change schools every few days. Most are war zones, but a few at the primary end manage for a week or two to dispel my fear – even, in the case of St Michael's School in Highgate, where I teach the son of Labour MP (later Chancellor of the Exchequer) Dennis Healey, providing whole days of not just relief but satisfaction.

Some of the children I encounter have left their imprint on the journal: five-year-old Alan, 'who looks as if butter wouldn't melt, but is constantly in trouble for stealing things'; Patsy, 'a pathetic youngster who can't stop washing her hands'; Steven Clutterbuck (I think I just liked the name), who has 'quaint little mannerisms'; Richard, son of an East German journalist employed by the *Daily Worker*, 'who spends his time making grotesque figures out of plasticine';

the sons and daughters of Jewish and other refugees from the Nazis; children whose parents have fled from the more recent war in Cyprus; the curly-headed offspring of West Indian immigrants, brought to England to do the jobs their white counterparts considered beneath them … What I wouldn't give to know what became of these children whose lives for a nanosecond touched mine.

I stay in the teaching job till we leave for the Continent prior to flying back to New Zealand. I credit those five months teaching children of people who were mostly at the bottom of the social heap with my *true* conversion to socialism. Had I the power, I would abolish private education altogether (Harold Wilson, when he became prime minister in 1964, had the same dream, but he failed to make it a reality). A two-tier education system means a two- or three- or four-tier society, not as a consequence of the inevitable differences between people, but as a result of institutional unfairness. In our neo-liberal, market-driven age, this sounds ludicrously naïve, but I hold to my conviction that only when the very best education is made available to every child in the land will a just and healthy society come into being.

* * *

Do I realise, as the first nervous signs of spring appear in parks and gardens, that our days in England are numbered? Did we talk about 'going home'? We must have, but I have no memory of it. What I feel – what I want to believe perhaps – is that my husband was offered a job, the kind he couldn't refuse, in Auckland, and that was the trigger. But I have no proof that this is how it was.

I'm taking lessons after school hours with Cicely Berry, the now celebrated RSC (Royal Shakespeare Company) voice coach. She encourages me to be serious about an acting career. At the same time we are having discussions with our neighbours from Redcliffe Gardens, Mike and Chris (Mike is English, Chris a refugee who fled Germany after her mother was raped by Russian soldiers), about travelling overland with them to India. Mike and Chris want to emigrate to Bombay. They want to put Europe and its wars behind them. The journey would take us through Greece, Turkey, Syria, Persia (Iran), Afghanistan and

Pakistan. Were we serious about doing this? If we were, the decision to return to New Zealand must already have been made. I search the journal for clues. 'I used to feel I wanted to live here but living in North London has convinced me that New Zealand offers more opportunities to lead a full life ...' Again I don't recognise the person who wrote that. What did she mean by 'a full life'?

The cold, dark days of winter have been enlivened by visits to the theatre and to hear concerts at the Albert and Festival Halls. Leonard Bernstein conducting and playing the Ravel Piano Concerto gets a rave in the journal, as does Paul Scofield (on whom I had an enormous crush) playing Lear. I can still hear his anguished howl on discovering the body of Cordelia. We've seen Dorothy Tutin and Ian Holm as the lovers in *Troilus and Cressida*; watched Spike Milligan behave anarchically in *The Bed Sitting Room*; roared with laughter as Jonathan Miller and Alan Bennett satirise the British establishment in *Beyond the Fringe*. On my return to England at the end of the decade some of these people would become friends, but if anyone had told me that at the time I'd have said they were dreaming.

The truth, I suspect, is that I was sleep-walking my way through those last months in London, escaping the dreary bed-sit, the scary job, the rubbish-strewn streets of Archway, the journeys on the frequently broken-down Northern Line, by creating an alternative universe. Perhaps my husband was sleep-walking too, seeing in a return to New Zealand *his* chance to escape from his dull job as a solicitor. For a few brief, happy weeks he'd worked as a legal journalist, filing pieces for the *Guardian*. His dream job. But the pay, like the work, was unreliable, so he gave it up. He once joked that he'd become a lawyer because of the film *Witness for the Prosecution*. Now here was his chance – an offer to join a top Auckland law firm, not as a jobbing solicitor but as a barrister – to *be* the crusading lawyer he'd so admired.

The overland adventure is scuppered when Mike learns he can't take his car into India. So another adventure is posited. We will spend three months exploring the Continent, then, thanks to an invitation from my school friend Janet, fly home via America. It's what happens, but it doesn't feel like the real story. Something is missing. If this were fiction, I would say the missing element is motivation. Assuming the job offer in Auckland was my husband's motivation, where was mine? I don't have an answer to that question. Memory, like the journal, is silent.

A week before we leave England I get a phone call from my agent. On the basis of my few television appearances he has secured me a part, subject to a satisfactory interview, in a play to be put on at the Bromley Repertory Theatre prior to a West End transfer. I tell him I can't do it. In fact there's no point him keeping me on his books, as I'll be living on the other side of the world. He expresses regret. Tells me this would have been my Big Break. I try not to believe him.

# Chapter Eight

The fourth of June 1963. I'm sitting in the minivan on the wharf at Dover waiting for the ferry to take us to Calais. I'm reading the *Sunday Times* and the *News of the World*. My husband is reading the *Observer* and the *Daily Mail*. We'd agreed it was important to see what was being said at both ends of the political and social spectrums. The *Observer* headline is 'PROFUMO RESIGNS'. The *Sunday Times* reads, 'A GREAT TRAGEDY FOR THE PROBITY OF PUBLIC LIFE IN BRITAIN'. John Profumo, the secretary of state for war, married to the actress Valerie Hobson, has been caught with his pants down. The woman in question is Christine Keeler, a high-class call girl who, while having an affair with Profumo, was also involved in a relationship with Yevgeny Ivanov, a naval attaché at the Russian embassy in London. But Profumo hasn't resigned because of a sexual misdemeanour, or because of a perceived threat to national security (the Cold War is getting colder); he's resigned because he lied to parliament.

'SKELETONS IN MANY CUPBOARDS', the *Daily Mail* proclaims, ratcheting up the excitement. So there's more to come ... Watching the British Establishment squirm as the goings-on at Cliveden, stately home of Profumo's friend Lord Astor, are made public, is the best fun I've had in ages. So much has been written the people involved are beginning to feel like distant, disgraceful cousins. Stephen Ward, the man at the heart of the story – he procured Christine Keeler for both Profumo and Ivanov – is a society osteopath and occasional artist (a portrait of Princess Margaret bears his name). He happens also to be an old boy of the minor public school my husband went to, a fact which brings the players in this drama even closer. The story of Ward's arrest, subsequent trial for 'immorality offences' and eventual suicide will follow us as we clatter our way around Europe, sleeping in the van when it's raining (as it frequently is), pitching our tent when it's dry, cooking meals on my trusty Woolworth's burners, our only regular indulgence being the purchase of English newspapers – the 'Profumo Affair' has us hooked – and coffee, which we drink while we read.

Politics has never been more exciting. Earlier enthusiasms – attending fundraisers in support of Franco's political prisoners; joining a picket outside the South African Embassy; gate-crashing an Oswald Mosley meeting out of sheer curiosity – can't compete with this heady mix of politics and sex.

'The Establishment will have to find someone to blame,' my husband insists. 'Ward was their delivery boy. He was bringing them exactly what they wanted. But he's not top drawer, so he's dispensable. Do you believe the story they're telling? That he led a good man to ruin? I don't.'

'Are they really that ruthless?'

'Are you really that naïve?'

We learn of Ward's suicide while sitting in a café on the Champs-Elysées. Our last few days on the Continent. Rain sloshing down.

'Wouldn't rush to judgment if I were you,' my husband mutters. 'Suicide? How convenient.'

'What do you mean?'

'Trial was almost over. Even a hostile judge was going to have difficulty making the charges stick. Why would Ward suddenly –'

'You're saying somebody killed him?'

'Wouldn't be the first time MI5 has tidied things up for the government.'

We had come full circle, and so had the story of Profumo. Two months later Prime Minister Macmillan will resign, bringing the whole sorry saga to an end.

Only it isn't an end. In 2014 the case is referred to the Criminal Cases Review Commission. At the time of writing no conclusion has been reached, but at least the right question is being asked: did Stephen Ward commit suicide, or was he murdered on the orders of MI5? (A question I still ask about the death in 2003 of another scapegoat – David Kelly, former UN weapons inspector in Iraq.)

* * *

I'm nearing the end of the journal. From here on, apart from the few weeks we spend in the States, I will be flying blind. In mostly uninspired prose laden with information gleaned from guidebooks, the journal has described the towns, villages, churches, monuments and museums visited on that three-month European odyssey. It recorded encounters with fellow holiday makers in camping grounds ranging from the semi-luxurious (Austria, Switzerland) to the rat-infested (Yugoslavia). It told of late-night conversations in Spoletto with de-Nazified Italians, anxious to impress upon us their great love for the English. It waxed lyrical about seeing – as much as we could from the cheapest seats at the back – *Aida* at The Baths of Caracalla in Rome, and Molière's *L'Avare*, starring the famous Jean Vilar, at the Papal Palace in Avignon. The week we spent camping on the beach at Almuñecar merited several pages; the times when I singed my hair cooking over the burner, or cut my hand trying to open a tin of baked beans, a sentence here and there.

Spain made a lasting impression on us. The poverty was shocking; the heat unbearable; Franco's armed guardia in constant attendance, appearing out of nowhere when we stopped to admire the view or picnic on the roadside. But something about the dusty beauty of the interior and the rocky grandeur of the coast (places favoured by the English were given a wide berth) affected us in profound and often surprising ways. Every evening at Almuñecar we watched chanting fishermen pull in their nets, then joined them later in the local café to drink rough red wine and listen to their haunting music. France was all rain and chateaux, sodden sleeping bags and angry farmers chasing us away from their fields, but Spain, for all its suffering under the yoke of Franco, touched our hearts.

Other countries enchanted or appalled according to how we experienced them. Places where the van broke down – as it did several times – were judged by how easily and cheaply it could be fixed. I didn't much like Germany, but I liked Austria, which reminded me of the South Island. Italy, with its art and its Catholicism and its crazy drivers, gave rise to a whole new set of clichés, as did both Denmark and Sweden, for different reasons. Just as in London, reminders of the war were everywhere – bombed buildings, gun emplacements, tangles of barbed wire, crowded cemeteries. We got lost in West Berlin. I nearly got arrested in East Berlin because I didn't have the right documentation (the 'paper tyranny of Communism'). Finally, clutching our newspapers, counting out our few remaining coins, we took the ferry back to England. Two weeks later we were on our way 'home' to New Zealand.

# Chapter Nine

'Give me your tired, your poor, your huddled masses yearning to breathe free …' Carved into the pedestal on which the Statue of Liberty stands, the words are so familiar as to be almost leached of meaning. I stare at the gigantic torch-bearing figure above me, and I think of the friend whose generosity has made this interlude between Europe and the reality of 'going home' possible. I met Janet in 1957 in my final year at school in Dunedin. She was in New Zealand for a year as an AFS (American Field Service) student. We quickly became, and have remained, friends. Without her offer to orchestrate our visit, arranging accommodation either with other AFS families or in cheap hostels, this three-week adventure would never have happened. We were broke. Now, reading the journal with its sanitised entries, I realise how significant this journey was. My husband fell in love with America. He wished he'd been born there. I did not.

We do the usual tourist things – Empire State Building, Staten Island, Statue of Liberty, the Guggenheim, two plays on Broadway, the Metropolitan Museum of Art. I have faithfully trudged around art galleries and museums in Europe, but I am struck dumb by Salvador Dali's 'Crucifixion'. Why this painting, which I no longer particularly like, should have blown the scales from my eyes, and not the Rembrandts in the Rijks Museum or the Goyas in Toleda, is a mystery to me. But here I am, tears running down my face as I contemplate the suffering of Christ on the Cross. What till now had been merely symbolic is suddenly, shockingly, real. From this moment on I look at paintings in the same way I read books, gripped (or not, as the case may be) by the stories they tell. Needless to say, the journal makes no mention of this epiphany.

We walk the streets of New York, joining the crowds the journal describes as 'little ants bustling about at the foot of a concrete ant heap', imbibing the atmosphere of a city that seems to belong to a different century, if not a different planet, from shabby, down-at-heel London.

'I'd give my right arm to be a citizen of this country,' my husband announces, on one of these muscle-burning walks.

'What? ... You're joking!'

'Don't you feel it? The energy, the possibilities ...'

'They execute people here. How could you live in a country that does that?'

'If that's the worst you can say ...'

The journal, predictably, makes no mention of this prescient conversation. All it says is, 'I would hate to live in New York, hemmed in by concrete superstructures, walking always in the shade.'

But we agree about the friendliness of Americans, their generosity and idealism. Kennedy is president. The Peace Corps is carrying the American dream to some of the poorest people in the world. And we agree that the future is here, and not in poor old bombed-to-bits Europe. 'After the cynicism and self-examination of England it's refreshing to be among people who don't have difficulty saying they believe in God, and the ideals of the Constitution ...' – I read those words and feel the familiar disconnect. My recollection of this time, and of the years that follow, is that I was living in that mental space, fast becoming fashionable, in which God is deemed to be dead. If I went to church at all it was because of a wedding or a christening, or as part of what was expected at Easter and Christmas. No one I knew, apart from my new American friends, talked about God.

Of course I knew there was a dark side to America, but in New York and the other cities we visit it was hidden from me. When, in Washington, we witness a debate in the Senate, chaired by Ted Kennedy, about the supposed communist content of certain American folk songs (the McCarthy era may have ended, but the anti-communist crusade is ongoing), we find it hilarious. But I have only to think of the difficulty I had getting a visa to come to the States at all – my China-based relative, Rewi Alley, was cited as evidence against me – to be reminded of the danger of being different in this New World utopia. To secure my visa I had to sign a document promising not to engage in political activity while I was in the United States. If I hadn't already embraced socialist ideals, that encounter with a nervous super-power would have ensured that, for the rest of my life, I would be on the side of the 'huddled masses'.

After New York and Washington we visit Boston, Chicago, Denver, Salt Lake City, San Francisco. Memory tells me that as the day of our return to New Zealand grows closer, so too does my sense of dread. What will I do with myself once we're back? I assume I will work, but at what? So far as I know there isn't a professional theatre in Auckland. And television is barely off the ground. The more I try to imagine Auckland, the more foreign it seems. Apart from my in-laws I know almost no one. Where will we live? ... The journal stays silent.

# Chapter Ten

In her 1935 novel, *Lucy Gayheart*, Willa Cather wrote, 'Some people's lives are affected by what happens to their person and their property; but for others fate is what happens to their feelings and their thoughts.' Stepping off the plane at Whenuapai airport, walking across the tarmac (as you did back then), breathing in the humid, mangrove-scented air, to be greeted in the terminal building by two sets of in-laws standing as far away as possible from one another, it's feelings and thoughts that overwhelm me, not the prospect of the comfortable life I have been promised. In this country, in this city, we are the lucky ones. We have health, prospective wealth, family support and university qualifications. 'We've made a mistake,' I whisper to my husband.

He squeezes my hand in what I take to be agreement.

The weeks that follow are a blur. Conversations, charged with the same pent-up emotions I experienced on arrival, last into the small hours. As people do when struggling to adjust to unpalatable truths, we talk in circles till either exhaustion or sleep shuts us up.

By Christmas I am back on the payroll of the New Zealand Broadcasting Service, President Kennedy has been assassinated, and we are living in a flat in Takapuna.

* * *

Programme Officer. That is my official title. It's a step up from Transcription Officer, but a thousand miles from what I would like to be doing. Choosing music for *Hawaiian Half Hour* strikes me as requiring almost as few brain cells as tying parcels. But I'm prepared to concede it *is* more interesting, not because of the work, but because of the people I'm working with. In the breaks for morning and afternoon tea I fall into conversation with people who know about music – serious music, not the Hawaiian variety. Soon conversation is replaced by demonstration as my new friend Terry invites me into one of the booths (used to test-drive the music we plan to programme) to hear the Swingle Singers, Joan Sutherland singing Lucia, my first counter tenor, a pirated record of Tom Lehrer songs ...

Terry is different. He has an encyclopaedic knowledge of music which he flaunts at every opportunity. He's opinionated, flamboyant, defiant of authority. As a result he has few friends in an organisation not known for encouraging criticism from within. He is also gay, though I don't know this yet. I find him fascinating, but instinct tells me he's not someone I should invite home to dinner.

A routine is established. Every weekday morning my husband and I leave our Takapuna flat (a minute's walk from the beach), drive over the new harbour bridge with all the other North Shore commuters, disappear into our respective places of work, then drive back at the end of the day. I think of myself as a good wife, a good hostess to our new circle of friends, a good daughter-in-law when occasion demands. But the people I'm increasingly drawn to are like Terry, people I can't invite home.

* * *

I have been living this new life for several months when a colleague to whom I have confessed my thwarted ambition to act tells me about Central Theatre, at the time the closest thing to professional theatre in Auckland. Central is the brainchild of Mary Amoore, a talented, driven woman, whose productions are already being cited as evidence that the city is more than ready for its own professional company. I contact Mary, do an audition, and wake next morning to find myself a member of a semi-professional organisation committed to staging everything from Shakespeare to Ionesco. Like all the other actors associated with the company, I keep my day job. I won't be cast in every show so there will be times when I'm not 'working' at all. When I'm employed, rehearsals will be in the evenings and at weekends.

Over the next few years I will play a number of leading roles: Sheila in Peter Nichols' *A Day in the Death of Joe Egg*, Katherine in *Henry V*, Mordeen in John Steinbeck's *Burning Bright*, Carol in Peter Shaffer's *Black Comedy*, Doreen in his *The Private Ear and the Public Eye*, the title role in Euripides' *Medea*, as well as many minor roles. These extra-curricular activities are, for the most part, ignored by my husband and his family – but this changes when, in May 1968, the fully professional Mercury Theatre opens its doors and I am hired to be part of the company. By then it's not just me who has changed, it's the world.

A lot has been written about the 1960s. Some see its celebration of permissiveness as a harbinger of neo-liberalism and the free market. Others blame it for the advent of the 'me' generation. I view it more tolerantly as a time when many went astray, but just as many found themselves by embracing new freedoms. You could say we were guinea pigs, trying out the pill and testing, under the new dispensation, the limits of flirtation, drinking alcohol every day instead of just at weekends, being offered a reefer or a hash cookie at parties. Inevitably some came unstuck. I could claim to be one of them, but that would be to deny my culpability. I did come unstuck, but not because I took drugs or drank too much. I became unstuck because I lost my way. Or, more accurately, I became unstuck because I had absolutely no idea what my way was.

Over the years I've searched for evidence that what happened to me, as to so many of us who were young at the time, can be explained (excused?) by what was going on in the world around us. But the truth is, while I thought I was conscious of the movements of history – this was the decade of the Vietnam War after all – like most of my contemporaries I was just getting on with my own life while listening, with increasing unease, to the voice in my head that told me something was terribly wrong. Then, in the middle of the decade, my daughter is born, and everything, except that pesky undermining voice, changes.

In November 1966 the country goes to the polls. The Vietnam War has caused a schism in New Zealand's outwardly homogeneous population that will be echoed (and magnified) fifteen years later when the Springbok rugby team arrives in the country. I attend demonstrations against the war, wheeling my daughter in her push-chair in the company of other young mums. The largest demonstration happens when US President Lyndon Johnson comes to Auckland to thank our government for its support of the war. There are scuffles and some arrests. It's suggested to me that I should think very carefully before exposing my daughter to such danger again.

On polling day I drive Labour supporters to the polls, unaware that a 'Vote National' sticker has been attached to the back window of my car. Does this mean what I think it means? How is that possible? It has to be a joke. That the man who converted me to socialism is now batting for the other team is simply not possible. Labour loses the election.

About this time I become a sleep-walker, a condition that plagued me through my childhood and teenage years. Several times a week I wander out of the bedroom of the faux colonial cottage we moved into before my daughter was born, waking, half frozen, curled in the foetal position in the far corner of the patio. I tell no one about this. Just as I tell no one about the voice in my head. Who, in any event, would I talk to? I would almost certainly have been told I had nothing to complain about. As for my faith – the Presbyterianism I was raised in as a child – that has gone the way of my belief in Romance and Happy-Ever-After. Not that I'm an atheist. I've never understood the appeal of a position that closes so many doors. But having stopped being a churchgoer, I can hardly turn to the church now for guidance. Only in work – by which I mean the theatre – do I find relief. Inhabiting another world, another persona, silences the voice in my head.

Unfortunately, theatre work is intermittent. There are months when I am simply a housewife – there was never any question, after my daughter was born, of my staying on at the NZBS – with nothing to do but play with my child and plan the next dinner party. Almost by default I begin studying. I have recently got to know John Reid, professor of English at Auckland University and a passionate advocate for theatre. He suggests I study for an MA, writing a thesis instead of sitting the full complement of papers, so I can do most of the work at home. With only a dim sense of the revelations that lie ahead I begin, under the direction of Allen Curnow, to read Yeats and Dylan Thomas. John Reid introduces me to contemporary American literature; Peter Dane to the tangled world of the metaphysical poets, seeding a lifelong fascination with the poet John Donne. Karl Stead supervises my thesis on the English theatre director and critic Harley Granville-Barker, the man who, with George Bernard Shaw, was responsible for the theatrical revolution of the early twentieth century. Two novels will come out of this intense period of study: my first, *Catch a Falling Star*, about John Donne; and my most recent (still to be published), *When We Were Lords*, celebrating the lives of the men and women who put the Royal Court Theatre on the map.

The crisis, for me, comes in the autumn of 1968. By this time no one can be in any doubt that the English-speaking world beyond our shores is in the throes of a social revolution destined to leave its mark on all future generations. The breaking down of sexual taboos, the availability of the pill and the re-emergence of feminist ideas have challenged traditional ideas of marriage and family. Homosexuality is still a crime, but my friend Terry doesn't stand out as he used to. He knows his time is coming. Being 'gay' is talked about more openly now. The use of code in books and films may still be necessary to get past the censor (in New Zealand in 1972 it was decreed, bizarrely, that because of the 'offensive language' in the film of James Joyce's *Ulysses* it could be shown only to gender-segregated audiences), but since we all knew what the various codes stood for, it was only a matter of time before the walls of censorship began to crumble.

The old world, with its lip-service to Christian values and its class distinctions, still stands (that word 'class' is not generally used in this country, but it's the right word to describe the social divisions in 1960s Auckland), but by 1968 the

Barbarians are rattling the gates. Television has proved a great leveller. Satirical shows from England, whether televised or seen live – *Cambridge Circus* tours New Zealand in 1964 – have outraged moralists reaching for the panic button. The launching of the magazine *Private Eye* in 1961, and the emergence in the theatre of the 'kitchen sink' school of dramatists, have raised the stakes even higher. New Zealand may be 12,000 miles away from where most of these things are happening, but it cannot escape the tsunami of change sweeping the globe.

1968 will go down in history as the year of the Mai Lai massacre in Vietnam, the assassinations of Martin Luther King and Senator Robert Kennedy, and the Russian invasion of Czechoslovakia. In my personal history it is the year my marriage ends and I move out of the cottage in Parnell to live with my daughter in an unfurnished flat in Kohimarama.

# Chapter Eleven

'Nothing could have been otherwise and life is a terrible thing'. The words are Oscar Wilde's, written after a visit to his wife's grave, following his release from Reading Gaol. Looking back on the months of anguish and guilt that followed the ending of my marriage, I find myself turning those words of Wilde's over and over in my mind. I will never stop regretting the pain I caused, but I could not have done 'otherwise'. 'Something was dead in each of us / And what was dead was Hope.'

At the request of my father-in-law I go to see his friend Fraser McDonald, the world-renowned psychiatrist and superintendent of Carrington Hospital. For an hour I sit opposite this good man who, with his wife, the artist Jacqueline Fahey, will become a lifelong friend, and weep. He hands me a box of tissues and says almost nothing till, red-eyed and embarrassed, I get up to leave. 'You must meet my wife,' he says. 'You two have a lot in common.' Many years later I learn that the phrase 'suburban neurosis', attributed to Fraser in his groundbreaking work as a psychiatrist, was in fact coined by Jacqui. 'There's nothing wrong with you,' Fraser says, as I turn from the door to thank him. 'You're not insane, just sad. That's what I'll be telling your father-in-law.'

Over the course of the next year I will work as a teacher, a kitchen hand at Auckland Hospital, an art gallery assistant and an actor. Money is scarce.

On one particularly grim day I walk out of the local fruit shop with a bunch of bananas – my daughter's favourite food – that I haven't paid for. I hurry away, expecting at any moment to feel a heavy hand on my shoulder. A hundred years earlier I would have been transported to the other side of the world for what I had just done.

Somewhere in the midst of this confusion I get myself a lawyer. Robert, a man of great kindness and a strong sense of justice, will also become a friend for life. Recently I asked him how he came to be my lawyer. I have no recollection of hiring him. 'You didn't,' he informs me. 'I was contacted by your husband's lawyer. He didn't feel comfortable with you not having legal representation, so he asked me if I would take you on as a client. I agreed.'

I owe Robert a great deal. Thanks to him I retained custody of my daughter, the one thing for which I would have fought, tooth and nail. I also retained control of my father's Trust, due to come to my brother and me on our mother's death, thwarting a move to have it made over for my daughter's sole use. That my father's money should be denied to me or to any other children I might have was, in Robert's view, one concession too many. I had already agreed to accept the minimum in child support, and undertaken not to contest the situation regarding what I had thought was a shared family home. It wasn't. It had never been put in our joint names. Seven years later the Property Relationships Act, enshrining the principle of equal division of property when couples separate, would come into force, but in 1968 there was no such protection.

Eventually I escape – that's how it feels – and move with my daughter to Rotorua, where a job has been offered to me in a local art gallery. It's not just the pressure of earning a living as a solo mother in a city where I have begun to feel like a pariah that is driving me south, it's the fallout from a relationship that began a few months after the separation. The man, who will become my second husband, is a New Zealand actor based in London. He has returned to this country to be with his dying father. Our relationship has been fraught from the start. There are other girlfriends, there is a problem with money (he seems to have even less than I have), I have a child whom he shows no interest in meeting, and I am still grieving the failure of my marriage. So when the offer of a job away from Auckland is followed by a letter offering accommodation from the aunt who twice rescued my brother and me when our mother was hospitalised, I don't hesitate. I know the risk I'm taking. I could lose the man I'm convinced I've fallen in love with. But the urge to be somewhere else, anywhere else, is too strong to resist.

Driving to Rotorua with my daughter and all my worldly possessions (including Felix the cat) piled into my ancient Ford Anglia, I seem to pass my younger self driving in a similarly overloaded car in the other direction. I push the image away. I can't think about the past or the future, I can only think about the next few months. I'm to live in a flat in the basement of my aunt's house. I'll be working three days a week in a small art gallery. I'm determined to do everything I can to forget the city I'm running away from, and the man.

'Yuk! What's that smell?' my daughter complains, as the smoky waters of Lake Rotorua slither into view.

I laugh. 'You'll get used to it, darling,' I answer her.

* * *

I stay in Rotorua for six months. For the second time in my life, the town that smells of rotten eggs becomes a place of transit. I would describe myself during much of this time as numb. I look after my daughter, I go to work, I see my old friends from NZBS days, I have Sunday lunch with my aunt and uncle, I walk and walk ... Then, about four months into my stay, the relationship I'd fled from takes a turn for the better. Bruce (I will be writing about this relationship only in the broadest terms, but not to use his name seems coy) visits for the weekend. I visit him in Auckland. By the time he's due to head back to England we have made plans for a shared future. Years later, Bruce will tell me that at the time of my flight to Rotorua there was a rumour going around that, despite my current impecuniousness, I was an heiress and would one day be a very rich woman. This, he cheerfully admitted, made me a great deal more attractive in his eyes.

I return to Auckland to live briefly with my soon-to-be mother-in-law. I'm to be divorced for adultery. How this came about is not a story for here. Suffice it to say that agreeing to be the guilty party was the only viable course of action open to me. I hunt out my copy of Hawthorne's *The Scarlet Letter*. Is this really who I am? The relationship with Bruce began after I separated from my husband. Surely that means it's not adultery? But apparently it is, technically, legally. If I want to start my new life and not wait seven years for the divorce to go through, this is the path I must go down.

'I know not whether Laws be right / Or whether Laws be wrong,' Wilde wrote from his prison cell. The law that decreed I was wholly to blame for the failure of my marriage was the one in place at the time. I had no choice but to accept its ruling. I didn't have to attend the court hearing. I was grateful to be spared that. But judgement can be a two-edged sword. I was judged as an adulteress, so I, in turn, judged the society that condemned me. I vowed never to live in New Zealand again.

# Chapter Twelve

Sitting next to my daughter as the plane climbs into the night sky, the scattered lights of Auckland yielding gracefully to the darkness of the Pacific, the emotion I am most conscious of is relief. Relief at leaving the disgrace of adultery behind; relief that the painful farewells to friends and family are over; relief that, at last, I am on my way back to England, to the start of a new life.

'A divorce is like an amputation. You survive but there's less of you.' Margaret Atwood hadn't written those words when I left New Zealand in 1969, but a few years later those were the words I wrote down when I read her novel *Surfacing*, half believing that they'd been written for me. By that time the enormity of what I had left behind – the country and the people amputated from my world – had begun to shape my thoughts and colour my dreams. The life I live, first in London, later in the Cotswolds and Oxford, is bracketed by reminders of New Zealand. In pride of place in each of the houses I live in is a painting of New Zealand bush by Dennis Knight Turner, purchased from the gallery I worked at in Rotorua. I decorate walls with prints by Don Binney, Michael Smither, Pat Hanly. I discover a print of Cook's iconic map of New Zealand and get it framed. Len Castle spice jars line my kitchen shelves; tie-dyed cloths brighten up faded sofas and chairs; kete hang in hallways; my father's collection of books about Otago, along with other accounts, historical and contemporary, of New Zealand, fills a bookcase; novels by the two Maurices, Shadbolt and Gee, share shelf space with other emerging New Zealand novelists. My children will tell me of their growing awareness that there was something strange about their lives, talking the local dialect at their village school, then coming home to a house filled with reminders of a country some of their friends hadn't even heard of, with, as like as not, a visiting Kiwi or two as house guests. Was there less of me as a result of my divorce not just from my husband but from the land of my birth? Perhaps that's why I'm writing this memoir: to retrieve what was lost; to heal that amputation.

* * *

If this were a romantic novel, I would be writing that I flew straight to England, my eagerness to be reunited with my lover acting as a tail wind, urging the plane on to its glorious destination. But though I was still a romantic, at least in my more confident moments, I'd learned something in the last decade that had changed the way I looked at the world. It was a lesson I'd learned in primary school when my friend Jennie defied the edicts of the class gang and invited me, the outsider, to play with her. Friends, I learned that day, could make the difference between hope and despair. It was something I'd almost lost sight of in Auckland when, in the wake of my separation, friendships changed, a precious few becoming stronger, but others fatally weakened by my decision to leave not only my marriage, but the social milieu in which it existed.

So here we are, mother and daughter, en route to England, our immediate destination not London but San Diego, California. My friend Jocelyn, daughter of Margot and Angus, is living there with her scientist husband. I would have stopped to see her anyway. San Diego is only an hour's flight from Los Angeles where, if flying direct, we would have needed to change planes. But Jocelyn has just lost a child – her second son, Toby – in a cot death. So I'm not just paying a quick visit, I will stay as long as she needs me.

I stay a week. Jocelyn is brave, dignified in her grief, and more beautiful than I have ever seen her, her eyes luminous with suffering, her glorious auburn hair worn in a long pigtail. She seems to me to be quite shockingly alone. Her husband's way of dealing with his grief is to shut himself away in his laboratory – though perhaps he is simply contriving to give two old friends time to themselves.

With the children – Jocelyn's and mine – in tow, we take the car over the border to Mexico, a day of distraction from grief, and from the yawning chasm of the future. Tijuana, known at the time as the murder capital of the world, acts on us both like a drug. Whatever anguish we had brought with us is overwhelmed by the kaleidoscope of colour and noise confronting us. One minute we're staring at a baroque church, all angles and angels and pale-pink stone, the next we're at a rundown dive selling tequila and Mexican chocolate stout. Horses jostle with cars. Men in wide hats, women in flaring multi-coloured skirts, dark-haired children seemingly unaware they are living in such close proximity to danger, gather and separate as if in response to commands from a dance master no one can see. It is both beautiful and terrifying.

The day we leave San Diego I'm unable to hold back tears. Jocelyn comforts me, which is not how it should be. It will be eleven years before I see her again.

We fly to Albuquerque, New Mexico. My friend Janet, who six years ago made those life-changing weeks in the US possible, is now living in Santa Fe. Her husband Nick is a scientist at Los Alamos, home to the National Laboratory where the atom bomb was designed. One day we drive up the winding mountain road that leads to Los Alamos so we can see where Nick works. As the town looms into view I have the uncanny feeling I've left the twentieth century and arrived in an Orwellian vision of the future. Churches – more per head of population than almost any other place in America – stand cheek by jowl with buildings in which the most terrible weapons in the history of the world are still being designed and built. I see mothers with children, but almost no men. They, presumably, are all working behind the heavily guarded doors of the laboratories. No wonder Nick chooses to live an hour's drive away from this surreal universe.

Being with Nick and Janet I'm reminded of how uncomfortably my instinctive liking for Americans (the most generous people in the world) co-exists with my equally instinctive mistrust of American power and policies. In San Diego Jocelyn took me to see the armada of mothballed ships, relics of both the European and Korean wars, moored in the US naval docks, a sight as weird as anything in science fiction. Now I learn that the beautiful mountains – the Sangre de Christo (Blood of Christ) – visible from the deck of Janet's Santa Fe home, are part of a mountain range pockmarked with old salt mines whose function, in this atomic age, is to store plutonium and nuclear waste.

Suddenly I am back at the day, seven years earlier, when I thought the world was going to end. It was at the height of what is now referred to as the Cuban Missile Crisis. For forty-eight hours I, like everyone else living in the northern hemisphere, braced myself for a nuclear attack. Of course it was scary, but it was something else as well, something I hadn't experienced before in London. I felt *connected*. No one was immune from the threat, so all were equally at risk. The sense of being in it together was palpable. London stopped being the loneliest city in the world and became a place where strangers unburdened themselves to one another. Sitting on the tube you would suddenly find yourself holding hands with someone whose name you didn't know, whom you would almost certainly never see again. (The only other time I've experienced anything like this, apart from the odd occasion during the years when the IRA were planting bombs in London, was when Tony Blair was elected after years of Thatcherite rule. The *Guardian*, describing it as a 'velvet revolution', recorded that the English were celebrating as only the English can – 'people travelling on the tubes made eye contact. Some even went to far as to smile ...')

By 1969 the Cuban Missile Crisis is far enough in the past to be dismissed as a near-run thing. But the nuclear threat is still real. The Vietnam War is still raging. And now I have a child. The thought of losing her to a nuclear bomb is far worse than anything I've imagined. I've seen the film *Hiroshima Mon Amour*. I know what a nuclear bomb can do.

'So now Tricky Dick is the man with his finger on the red button,' I say to Nick. 'How do you feel about that?'

Nick, a man with large feet of clay whom I have grown to like a lot, gives me one of his enigmatic smiles. 'Ah well, you see, that's the beauty of the American system. It throws up a Kennedy one year, a Nixon the next. You have to take the rough with the smooth.'

I wasn't sure I understood him (though when I think that George Bush was followed by Barack Obama, then Obama by Donald Trump, perhaps I do). Nick is often hard to understand, not because he's so much brighter than most people, but because he lives in a world shaped by paradox (dropping the atom bomb to bring about peace). Of white Russian extraction, Nick's hatred of communism borders on the paranoid, but that doesn't stop him being opposed to the war in Vietnam or, years later, expressing his disgust with Obama for his failure to punish the bankers responsible for the financial collapse of 2008. But in 1969 what is preoccupying him is the changing of the guard at Los Alamos. In place of the free exchange of ideas – the atmosphere that defined the Oppenheimer era – there has been an increase in bureaucratic control, with the result that the scientific community, instead of operating as a team, has been broken up into its component parts – engineers, computer scientists, chemists, physicists, biologists, mathematicians – all pursuing their own goals. Nick will stop working at Los Alamos in the mid-1980s. As a result of the experiments he and others conducted there he will go on to become one of the world's leading MRI (magnetic resonance imaging) scientists. The long winding road up the mountain to the town of churches and weapons laboratories is consigned to the past.

'When are you writers of fiction going to start dealing with the scientific world?' Nick will ask me on one of his rare visits to England. 'Don't you realise the power that sits in the hands of the men in white coats working away in their laboratories, any one of whom, if he was in possession of the right information, could bring New York to a standstill with a simple flick of a switch? Not all that difficult to cut power or water to a city. Not if you're a scientist. How about that for a story?'

I didn't have an answer. He was asking the wrong writer. (I'm getting ahead of myself here. In 1969 I'm not even imagining a life as a writer.) Nick's question, asked in the wake of the publication of my first novel, left me with a dismaying sense of how far my kind of writing was from the things that could alter our world in a heartbeat. While still at university I'd devoured the novels of C.P. Snow. His famous delineation of the worlds of Art and Science, with its implied criticism of those who saw them as opposites, had asked the same question. Yet here we were, a decade and a half after those novels were written, no nearer an answer. Literary fiction still tended to keep the laboratory at arm's length. Science, whether fictional or factual, remained the province of thriller writers and the followers of Arthur C. Clarke. I've never read science fiction. Like horror, it's a genre that holds no interest for me. At the time of my conversation with Nick I would probably have said I didn't read thrillers either. Why bother with a genre in which plot inevitably trumps character? But that was before I read John le Carré. I know better now. Le Carré's brilliant dissections of the world of power and politics, with its forays into the drug and arms trades, the uses and misuses of science, quickly overcame my snobbish resistance to the genre he has made his own. When Nick asked me why literary writers weren't dealing with the questions raised by science, I hadn't read le Carré.

* * *

The day comes when we must leave Santa Fe with its magical sunsets over the contaminated mountains and fly first to LA, then to Heathrow. Once again I will be arriving in England at the height of summer, only this time the sun will be shining.

We are to live, thanks to Bruce's chance meeting with a fellow Kiwi actor, in a flat in Marloes Road, Kensington. But we will not be on our own. We are to share with the actor and his English girlfriend. Bruce has no money. This is all he can afford. By the end of my first day I have discovered that not only does he have no money, he also has debts. I agree to pay them with the money I have brought with me from New Zealand. Once that's done, and a second-hand car has been purchased, I too am broke.

The summer of 1969 is one that will go into the record books. Not until 1976 will there be another like it. Each day seems warmer and sunnier than the one before. I sit in the garden of our neighbourhood pub, drinking wine, chatting to people who seem to have the world at their fingertips, and tell myself this is what I've been waiting for, this community of like-minded folk – artists and writers and musicians – eager to work and change the world. There's plenty of work to be had, too, even for actors. And when acting work dries up, there's a generous unemployment benefit. I don't know whether the West End dole office has been set up to deal specifically with artists, but it seems that way each time we show up for the weekly payout. There we are, in the heart of London's theatre land, rubbing shoulders with famous and not-so-famous names. Cash in hand, we repair to the nearby actors' pub for a beer and a ploughman's and the cheerful, mutual reassurances that the next job is just around the corner.

Sharing living quarters with another couple quickly brings home to me how finicky I can be when it comes to domestic life. My mother's training – cleanliness is, and always will be, next to godliness – has instilled in me a need to hunt out dirt in the farthest corners of cupboards and drawers and eliminate it. This is something of a mission in a flat that is in urgent need of TLC, having over the years seen many occupants, none of whom were brought up by my mother! I manage not to complain when I find myself washing my flatmates' dishes as well as my own, but a few days before we leave the flat for good, I lose my cool and say things I quickly regret. I'm forgiven, and we remain friends. Lesson learned.

* * *

Summer does eventually take its leave, but autumn, when it comes, brings more than just a change in temperature. Bruce is offered a four-month season at the Nottingham Playhouse. I don't have to be told what this means. The Playhouse is being described as 'the national theatre of the provinces'. Under the brilliant direction of John Neville it has brought works by Brecht, Gogol, O'Casey, Wedekind and Gorki into the mainstream repertoire, creating, in the process, many of the stars of the future – Ian McKellen, Peter O'Toole, Judi Dench (whose performance as Shaw's Saint Joan received rapturous reviews). Ten years later Judi will write the foreword for a book celebrating thirty years of the Nottingham Playhouse. 'It was so exciting to be working in a new theatre with a really great and enthusiastic group of actors. I never remember empty seats in the theatre at all – I am sure this isn't an exaggeration – the foyer always seemed full from early morning to late in the evening, with people meeting for coffee and drinks, seeing an exhibition, just coming in for a chat ...'

In 1969 John Neville is no longer at the helm but the new director, Stuart Burge, is creating almost as many waves. Who knows, there might even be work for me?

# Chapter Thirteen

We drive to Nottingham on a wet, prematurely freezing day in October, our car piled high with the things we will need for the next four months, our spirits even higher. Stuart Burge has made it clear he wants actors' families to feel at home in the theatre. Wives, husbands, children are welcome to attend rehearsals – no injunctions about noisy kids: parents are trusted to keep their offspring under control – or just hang about in the dressing rooms, café or bar. An impressive list of plays has been chosen: *King Lear*, with Michael Hordern in the lead role; a new play, *The Demonstration*, by David Caute; Brecht's *Arturo Ui*; *The Hero Rises Up* by John Arden and Margaretta D'Arcy. This is a theatre designed to change lives, not simply help pass the time.

Four months have passed since I arrived in England, but apart from our London flatmates I've made no new friends. It will take me a year or two to master the English way of friendship – not rushing in where angels fear to tread – and to feel the kind of connection I had with my New Zealand friends. But once I get the hang of things, the friends I make will be lifelong.

Nottingham will always be, for me, the place where the process of embedding myself in English life and culture really began. In the cheerfully chaotic atmosphere created by Stuart Burge, making friends comes easily. Stuart's vision of one big happy theatrical family must have had its cracks, but I never saw them. I have an instant rapport with the Australians in the company – another Bruce and his wife Helen. At the same time I fall under the spell of the brilliant and outrageously funny Donald and his equally brilliant wife Shirley – like me a full-time mum. In a few years she will become an internationally acclaimed writer. The camaraderie that develops will survive marital break-ups and global separations. When, three years after the Nottingham season, Bruce and Helen decide to return to Australia, I'm heartbroken. I write a poem, one of my first, titled 'Leftover Love', which I now can't find. But I can remember, as if the parting had only taken place yesterday, the feeling of desolation that overwhelmed me when we said goodbye.

Our first week in Nottingham is spent with a New Zealand family who take in boarders. By the end of the week I've found a flat. I couldn't be happier. At last we can live as a family. But there's a problem. Our landlady lives downstairs. Three days after we move in, she comes to me to complain about my daughter jumping on the bed. Apparently it disrupts the television reception. I apologise, and promise to make sure it doesn't happen again. But it does, when my back is turned, prompting a further complaint. This doesn't go down well with Bruce. He loses his temper, and we lose the flat.

The following day we move into a lodging house near the theatre. Living there already are several other members of the Playhouse company, including Penelope Wilton (later of *Downton Abbey* and *The Best Exotic Marigold Hotel* fame), a recent graduate from drama school. We become friends. (Three decades later, Penny will play a leading role in my BBC adaptation of Martin Boyd's *Lucinda Brayford*.) Living in a lodging house with half a dozen other, admittedly entertaining, people is not how I'd hoped to spend our time in Nottingham, but we're saving money, so I try to make the best of it. Then, just before Christmas, there's a breakthrough. A flat costing no more than we are already paying becomes available. It has only one bedroom, and I can smell the damp the moment I open the door, but to me it spells home. 'We'll take it,' I tell the landlord.

We move in on a day when there's barely enough daylight to distinguish it from the night, but it would take more than freezing fog to extinguish my excitement. We will have a family Christmas. I'll put up a tree. I'll make mince pies and Christmas pudding. I have my first dinner guest, Bruce's agent, Vernon. I like Vernon. He reminds me of Terry. Jewish and gay, he knows what it is to be an outsider. Sometime in the following year, by which time he has become a friend, I write a poem for him.

**For Vernon**

Whatever it is in you that answers
whatever it is in me,
that can't be named, that isn't love
(what has been lost maybe? Or
never found?)
that nods at sex, but isn't that,
that enables us to talk of God,
is sometimes so near,
so almost in the air,
I could cry to hear you say,
you feel as much as I,
whatever it is in you,
whatever it is in me,
will never die.

* * *

The planned Christmas doesn't happen. I fall ill. This tendency of mine to become sick when happy or excited has caused me much frustration over the years. In gloomy moments I tell myself it's because I don't deserve to be happy, but I know this is nonsense. Bruce calls a doctor who diagnoses rheumatic flu. 'You'll have aches and pains when you're middle aged,' he predicts cheerfully. 'Mind you, go on living in this slum, you might not even make it to middle age.'

Over the next few days I will see quite a bit of this doctor. Despite his dire predictions, I recover. I even start to like him. He speaks with an Etonian accent, yet his heart is clearly not with the class he was born into but with the poor, of whom there are many in the post-industrial Midlands. 'I despair of the middle classes,' he tells me on one of his visits. 'They're either aspiring to get a rung higher on the social ladder, or busy covering their tracks because they don't want anyone to know where they've come from. No wonder Cromwell's revolution failed.'

By the New Year I'm out of bed and living life again. Despite the gloomy weather I team up most days with Shirley and Helen, to pass the time and amuse our children. I've given up any thought of finding work. I'm out of my league here. How can I compete with actors who've had three years of RADA training? Gradually, so gradually I haven't noticed it happening, my confidence in my acting ability has been eroded. Bruce is not only RADA trained, he's in demand. How would it work if we both had jobs? I also have a sneaking suspicion he doesn't think much of my talent. He saw me play a variety of roles in Auckland but never passed any comment. If I asked him for an opinion his answers, invariably, were enigmatic. 'Well, it's a difficult play. You were brave to take it on.' 'It was the wrong part for you, Love. You'd have been better as ...'

But I'm not unhappy. I have friends now and a place I can call, for however short a time, home.

When it's not actually snowing or raining, Helen, Shirley and I organise chilly picnics among the ruins of Nottingham Castle or in nearby Wollaton Park. Wrapped in woolly hats and gloves, our noses red from the cold, we play hide and seek with the kids, jumping out like startled ghosts from behind broken pillars or trees shrouded in mist. Our shrieks of fright and laughter mimic the cawing of the crows wheeling above our heads. We're not on the Yorkshire moors, but that doesn't stop us pretending, when a dog starts howling in the distance, that we are in the presence of the Hound of the Baskervilles. Sometimes when we're in the park we see deer peeping out from the woods, curious as to who these creatures are, leaping about in the half light. We almost never see another

*Wedding day, with Uncle Charles and Aunt Betty.*

*Below: With my bridesmaids. From left: Fay (daughter of Betty and Charles), Jennie and Jocelyn.*

*The house at Lake Okareka.*

*Left: Twenty-first birthday weekend. On the lake with my cousin Ann (left).*

*With Digby Law (of cookbook fame) in* A Flea in her Ear *at Mercury Theatre.*

The Chalk Garden *at Rotorua Little Theatre, with Pearl Painton.*

*Above left: In Cairo with Tony and Jill.*

*Below left: A publicity photo for* Spotlight, *1963.*

*Opposite top: The Grand European Tour!*

*Opposite below left: Camping beside the Danube.*

*Opposite below right: With Janet and Nick in State College, Pennsylvania, on our way home to New Zealand.*

*Our home in Parnell.*

*Left: In* Medea, *an Auckland Central Theatre production, 1964.*

*Opposite: Graduation Day, 3 May 1953, Auckland.*

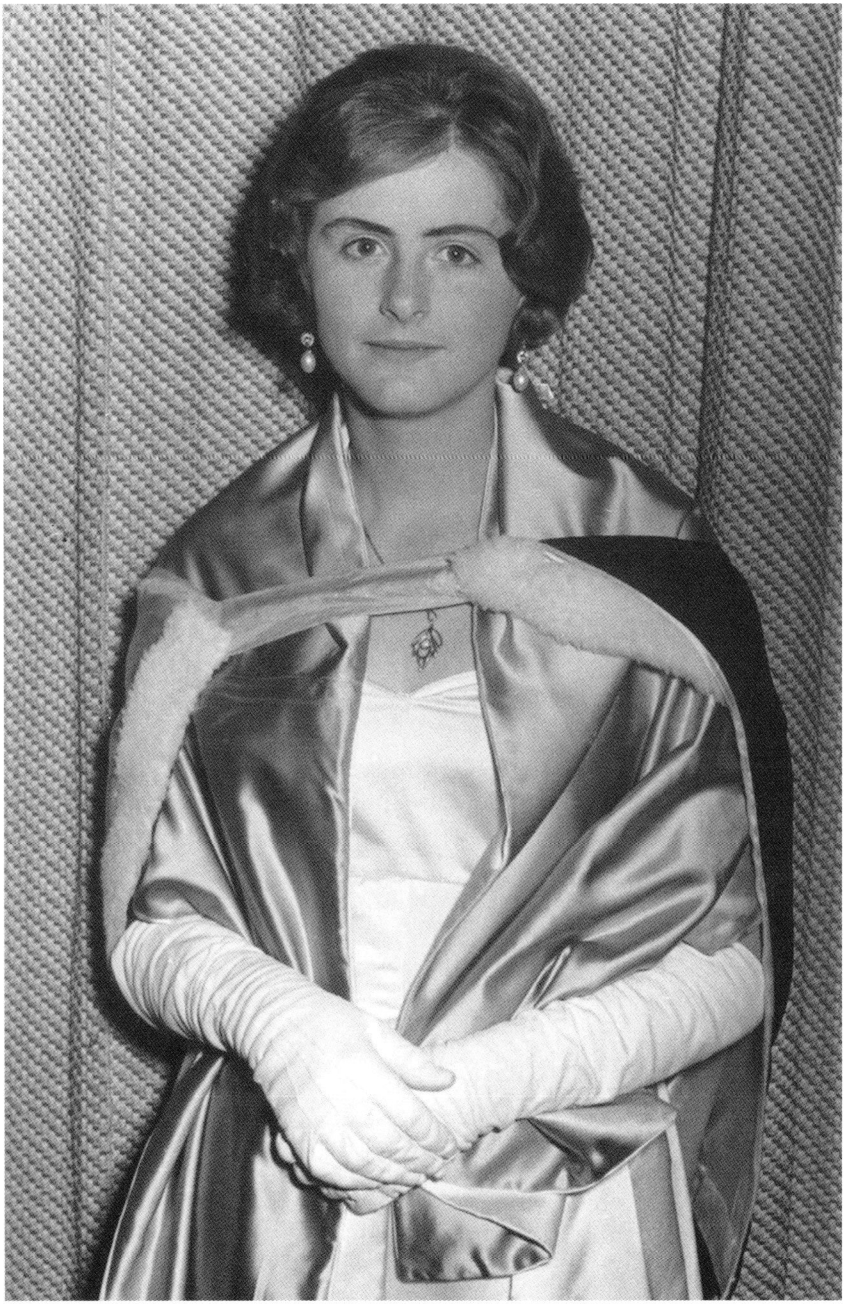

*Another wedding day, 11 February 1970, Marloes Road Registry Office in Kensington. From left: director Richard Martin Thomas, Bruce, and our flatmate Cindy.*

*Left: Our second London home, South Hill Park Gardens. Our flat was on the top storey.*

*The Long House.*

*The courtyard and stable of The Long House.*

*The courtyard in spring.*

*Top left: Best friends Mego the dog and Oddy the cat, both acquired soon after moving to The Long House. They died 16 years later, within two days of each other.*

*Above: Our horse Noggin making his way through the house from the stable.*

*Left: Riding my 1920s bicycle accompanied by Mego.*

*Carole – close friend, Long House neighbour and celebrated biographer.*

*Below: One of many Long House parties – Judi Binney on my right.*

*Sebastian Black and Judi Binney partying up.*

*Below: Another day, another Kiwi party on the lawn: Susie Lamb (front left), Michael Neill (standing at head of table), me (beside him), Sebastian Black (beside me).*

*At work on* A State of Blood *with Henry Kyemba (left) and John Man.*

*Below left: Alison and Ben Kingsley at the start of my working association with Ben.*

*Below: With John Hurt at an Ascott-under-Wychwood village cricket match.*

*Back in New Zealand on my brother Tony's farm.*

*A publicity photo taken in 1991 by my stepson Sean Shadbolt.*

human, although we do find a statue erected to the memory of the poet Byron's dog! Not for the first time I feel a thrill at this evidence of the past being close physically as well as imaginatively.

(Years later, living in New Zealand with Maurice Shadbolt, I will try to put this feeling into words. I'm attempting to explain my homesickness for England, a feeling Maurice regards as bordering on treasonable. 'I never felt alone when I lived there,' I tell him. 'Every time I walked down a country lane or along a cobbled street in London, I'd sense friendly ghosts walking beside me – lovers hurrying to illicit meetings, soldiers going off to war, mill workers stepping across stones laid centuries ago on sodden fields ...'

Maurice looks at me in astonishment. 'You're in love with dead things,' he accuses. 'No wonder you're so fucked up.'

'You can talk. You're always writing about the past.'

'Ah, but there's a difference. I'm not defined by it. I live in a country where you can still, if you're lucky, stumble on a beach that's never seen a human being before. There it is spread out before you. Like the Garden of Eden. Like the world has only just come into being. Not a ghost in sight.')

Ghosts or not, I loved Nottingham, a dark satanic city with a mind and heart of its own. I loved its sepulchral parks, its terraces of coal-blackened houses, its cobbled streets, its buses materialising out of the mist like growling behemoths. I loved being called 'Pet' and 'My Duck' by shopkeepers and bus conductors; loved the sense of community that developed not only with theatre folk but with the people I encountered in my daily life. Most of the people I met were, by New Zealand standards, impoverished. Life was hard, so pleasures, when they came, were seized on and celebrated. Despite the general greyness of the weather (well, it *was* winter), when I think back to this time I see patterns of streaky light, glimpsed through grubby windows or reflected in damp pavements, as if the sun had crept out of its prison for a few brief hours to remind us of its existence.

* * *

But the theatre remains the focus. On days when it's too miserable for picnics or trips to the playground, my new friends and I meet in the foyer of The Playhouse for coffee and cake, sneaking into rehearsals if the kids are quiet, surprising our partners at lunchtime with tea and sandwiches. Helen teaches me to knit. Completely lacking in talent, unable to follow the simplest pattern, all I can manage is a scarf. When I ask Helen to teach me how to cast off, she looks at Shirley, who grins, conspiratorially. 'Why stop?' she says. 'You're just getting going.' So the scarf grows and grows till, by the time we leave Nottingham, it stretches all the way round the auditorium. I leave it behind. For all I know it's still there, hidden away in the small room that used, in the bad old days, to house hundreds of unread play scripts.

Opening nights are the highlight. We three friends find babysitters, dress as if we're going to the Oscars, and wait nervously for the curtain to rise. Intervals see us slithering through the crowd, trying to gauge the mood of the audience. After the curtain call we wait excitedly in the bar for our partners. Love is in the air. We are as proud and full of chatter as peacocks. After so many domestic, child-centred days, we deserve this moment. It belongs to us as much as it does to the actors now walking, with beaming, freshly scrubbed faces, towards us.

* * *

The season ends in February. We return to London, to the flat in Marloes Road. Bruce and I are to be married. This is one of the conditions I had to agree to in the divorce settlement. I was never told why this clause was inserted, but I assumed it was to ensure my daughter was brought up in a 'respectable' household. Not that I objected, then or now. I was living a life that felt real. I can't say it felt safe – everything was too new for that – but it was safe enough for me to be confident about the future. 'I haven't been able to resist safety,' Saul Bellow wrote in a letter to a friend, 'and I haven't been able to rest in it.' Words I could have written myself back then. Safety had been sacrificed for adventure. And for something else. Writing. It had begun, almost in secret, soon after I made the decision to give up acting. By the end of our stay in Nottingham I'd completed a novel. *No Daffodils for Mrs Browning* – a title that owes a debt to Paul Gallico's *Flowers for Mrs Harris*, which I'd read as a teenager – is so thinly autobiographical it fooled no one who knew me, but it caught the eye of Vernon, who had begun to take on writers as well as actors. When he asked if he could represent me I thought he was joking. Luckily (I can say this now) the novel remains unpublished. A trendy new publishing house called Allison & Busby wanted it, but told me it was too short. Could I make it longer? I tried (of course I tried!), but I failed.

Recently, searching for something else among my ill-organised files, I found the manuscript of *No Daffodils*. I was so certain I'd lost it, I stared at the name on the cover for several seconds before plucking up the courage to start reading.

The first page is neatly typed, with Vernon's name and address in bold letters at the top. I start to read. A psychiatrist (male) has been asked to interview a young woman arrested on a charge of attempted murder. The story is being told in the first person, by the psychiatrist. There's a conversation with the defence lawyer who has hired him, followed by a visit to the family with whom the accused girl, out on bail, is living. I finish the chapter and shake my head in surprise. This isn't bad! I'm intrigued. I'd not thought of *No Daffodils* as a psychological thriller, but that's clearly what the first chapter is setting it up to be. I'd also forgotten that I'd written it in the first person, and that my protagonist is male. I would write from this point of view again, several years and several published novels later, and only then realise what a herculean task it is to pull off. But it seems, scribbling away in the chill of that Nottingham winter, I was blind to the difficulty of the form I had chosen. Ignorance really is bliss.

Now of course I can see what's wrong with the story. It's not just that it's too short – novellas were not fashionable in the early 70s – the language is clichéd, the tone too uniform. But I like it more than I thought I would. I'm not tempted to burn it (as I did with another later novel which then, equally mysteriously, turned up again, not among my own files but among the files of my current agent).

Encouraged by Allison & Busby's reaction, I start a second novel, *Whittaker Bay*. It too is strongly autobiographical, though this time it's not about my mother but about the life I lived in Auckland during my first marriage. I've hunted high and low for this novel but I can't find it. I know I didn't burn it! Perhaps it will turn up when this memoir is finished and I have no use for it. I still remember the highs and lows I experienced writing it, as if that lost domain was being restored to me not merely as the locus of a lived life, but as a place 'entire of itself', shrouded in the mystery that clings to all lost times and places. Vernon liked the book, but Allison & Busby turned it down, so it languished. It didn't matter. I was hooked. By sheer chance, I'd stumbled on the one life that, for all its vicissitudes, would never let me down – the life of the writer.

# Chapter Fourteen

I become a wife for the second time on 11 February 1970. A low-key ceremony at the Marloes Road Registry Office, followed by lunch in a pub. So now for the third time in my life I answer to a different name (though my birth name is still hidden from me). At least this time no one suggests changing my Christian name.

* * *

Seven years after that simple ceremony my name changes again, only this time I can't blame anyone but myself. I'm having lunch with the publisher of my first novel, *Catch a Falling Star*, a fictional account of the life of the Elizabethan poet John Donne, with whom I have been obsessed since reading him at university. The novel has come about as a result of a script I wrote for the BBC to commemorate four hundred years since Donne's birth. I had by this time established myself as a writer of radio plays for the BBC, but the Donne commission was an unexpected step up into the world of television. In the end the producers decided not to go down the fictional road, but my script somehow found its way into the hands of the publisher Anthony Blond, who then approached me to write a novel.

'So ... what name are you going to publish under?' Anthony asks me. 'Your married name?'

'Hadn't thought about it.'

'Well, I suggest you do, since you'll probably be stuck with it from now on. Don't imagine this is going to be your only novel … What's your maiden name?'

'Somerville,' I tell him.

'Hmm …' He gives me a look, as if he's trying to decide whether to make a pass or not. Anthony is something of a legend in the world of publishing. Irrepressible (his business partner, Desmond Briggs, would probably say *irresponsible*), with a reputation as a colourful man about town, he's just ordered a second bottle of wine. Not that there's anything unusual about this – liquid lunches were the order of the day in the literary world of the 70s – but to me it seems the height of decadence. 'Elspeth Somerville,' he muses. 'Bit of a mouthful after a glass or two. What's your middle name?'

'Sandilands,' I inform him. I'm struggling to hold back giggles. Raised in a teetotal house, I have a notoriously light head. Besides, I'm still dizzy with excitement at the prospect of being a published author.

'Curiouser and curiouser,' Anthony says, frowning. 'All those S's.' He wipes his mouth on his napkin.

I check my own mouth nervously. I live in the country. I have two young children. I wear hand-me-down clothes. Sitting opposite a man who appears regularly in the pages of *Vogue*, usually in the company of Lady Someone-or-Other, I feel like an imposter. When Anthony leans across the table to refill my glass I put my hand out to stop him.

'Tell you what,' he says. 'Let's shorten it. Elspeth Sand. How does that sound?'

I laugh out loud. I can hardly believe what I've just heard. One of my favourite fantasies about my birth centres on the novelist George Sand, Chopin's mistress. I know it's crazy, but she did have children, so it's possible – in my universe anyway – that I could be her great-great-great-granddaughter. Now here I am being offered her name as my own.

Only trouble is, I've misheard my Svengali host. He didn't say Sand, he said Sands. Which I will discover, nine months later when the novel comes out, he spells Sandys.

'I thought you said Sand. Singular,' I protest down the phone. 'Where did the y come from?'

'Class, dear girl,' he answers cheerily. 'It's the classy version. Now you can say you're related to Dirty Duncan.'

I don't have to ask him who he's referring to. Having lived in England in the early 60s, I know all about Duncan Sandys, the Conservative cabinet minister, son-in-law to Winston Churchill, who was rumoured to be the notorious 'headless' man cited in the Duchess of Argyll's divorce case – a scandal on a par with the Profumo Affair.

There's nothing to be done, of course. From now on, for better for worse, Elspeth Sandys will be my professional name. Two decades later, it will also become my legal name. But that's another story.

* * *

Thanks to my friends John and Shirley, who offer us their cottage in Devon, we're able to have a brief honeymoon. On a whim one day we drive across the Tamar River to take a look at Cornwall. Something happens to me almost the moment we leave Plymouth. As we wend our way along lanes never intended for cars, I glimpse, behind tangled hedges, fields vibrant with the green of early spring, curving across the land till, in a turn of the road, I see where they're headed – towards the unforgiving cliffs and a headlong tumble into the waves. I open the car window and there it is – the smell of the sea. It's the smell of childhood. Is that the source of my enchantment? The seagulls make the same melancholy sound as the gulls that swoop over the Andersons Bay inlet. Ragged stone walls snake across gorse-covered hills just as they do on the Otago Peninsula. Churches, their spires wreathed in mist – even the smallest village has one – multiply across the landscape, taking me back to the verandah of my family home in Dunedin where I would stand and count the steeples (some of which, I saw as I grew older, were not spires at all but chimneys) marching like good Christian soldiers all the way to the horizon.

But there is more going on than nostalgia. I breathe in the salty, wind-blown, bird-tossed air, and slowly, almost without noticing it, I fall in love. From this day on, I will return to Cornwall at every opportunity. It will become the place I go to when life overwhelms me. I take my children there for holidays, sometimes twice in one year. I will share it with my London-based cousin Gwynnedd (we drive along those skinny lanes with the windows down, singing at the tops of our voices the Presbyterian hymns of our shared childhood). Confident everyone will feel as I do about the place, I invite visiting Kiwi friends, as well as my new English friends, to join me for weekends and holidays. Almost the last thing Bruce and Helen and their children do before leaving for Australia is spend a week with me and my family in the rented cottage that has become my second home. I will write more poems about Cornwall's cliffs and caves, its sea-locked villages and Modigliani trees (battered to within an inch of their lives by Atlantic gales), its Celtic crosses, churches and sacred wells, than I will about anything or anywhere else. Had I known the Māori word tūrangawaewae, that is what I would have called Cornwall – my tūrangawaewae, the place where I stand.

One place in particular haunts me to this day – the abandoned church at Rame Head, home to birds and spiders and forgotten prayer books thick with dust. Miss Haversham's church, I say to myself, as the door I have had to force open slams shut behind me. Though I don't know it at the time, it will be the first of many visits. Why this place in particular should have got under my skin is not something I can easily explain. The tenacity of stone, perhaps? The tenacity of faith, of dreams? Standing in isolated grandeur on the edge of the cliff it would, in the not too distant past, have offered comfort and meaning to men and women whose lives were ruled by the relentless power of the sea and the lash of Atlantic gales. Now it offers only a sense of loss so vast it's as if Nature herself has been doomed to perpetual mourning. Eventually, of course – this is Cornwall: coastal erosion is endemic – the sea will win, and the church will disappear. Perhaps that's why I can't free myself of its power. I touch the wet stones and feel through my fingers what their fate will be. Pews and pulpit, stained-glass windows and spire, birds' nests and prayer books will sink forever under the indifferent waves.

**On Discovering the Church at Rame Head, Cornwall**

Miracle at first,
then mystery, then threat.
There was no way of preparing for it.
Sharp as acid, black as a wound, the
spire lunges out of the land, a
malevolent rocket programmed for God.

Inside, a candled silence, heavy with damp,
shadows twisting on cold stone aisles,
faded heraldry, a peephole to the pulpit, a
notice on the door for the protection of birds.
Sad-faced saints stare back at me,
pinioned like butterflies in the frozen light.

Outside again, wind grips,
earth squelches, sea-birds squawk,
broken monuments, masked with weed, snatch and tear.
I walk awkwardly, avoiding the spire.
Rain spatters the grey horizon,
clings to the ravelled trees like warm breath on window pane.
Ten centuries of human habitation – moss, mould, the wrenched grey stone.

The spire follows me, splintering the sky.

* * *

Miraculously, four weeks after that honeymoon visit I am back. An unexpected invitation to visit two people I met during my second, brief sojourn in Rotorua arrives at Marloes Road. Ken, a forestry scientist – he was in New Zealand as an adviser to the government – and his wife Meg are three decades older than I am, but the rapport that developed quickly obliterated any difference in age. I knew they came from Cornwall and that Ken was some sort of unofficial squire of his windy corner of England, but the information, at the time, meant little to me.

Now I stare at the address – 'Trewinney, Talland Bay, near Looe, Cornwall' – and my mind floods with the sights and sounds of the magical world glimpsed so recently on the other side of the Tamar Bridge. Bruce is in Edinburgh filming a TV series. There's nothing to stop me packing my bag and taking myself and my four-year-old daughter to Talland Bay.

We leave in winter and arrive in spring, such is the transformation from London to Looe, where our journey ends. Ken and Meg are there to meet us, two grey-haired sprites eager to show me as much of Cornwall as we can squeeze into three days. What follows is pure enchantment. It's not just the picnics on seaweed-strewn beaches (the four of us wrapped in winter woollies despite the daffodils in the garden and the lambs in the fields), or the cliff walks during which we gather sea spinach for our evening meal, nor is it the visits to smugglers' caves and abandoned tin mines, vivid those these experiences are. It's the house we're living in that sets the seal on my enchantment. Trewinney, Ken's family home, will change and grow in my imagination, appearing in my fiction as both a symbol of a world that will soon be gone forever (in one story Trewinney is sold to developers who knock it down and turn its gloriously overgrown garden into a caravan park) and a place where magic happens. Because magic did happen there. I saw it with my own eyes.

Our first night in the house I wake needing the bathroom. I go out into the corridor – Trewinney isn't vast, but it's big enough to get lost in – and feel my way towards where I think the bathroom is. Not finding it, I turn into another corridor where I'm met by a woman wearing a long white nightdress and a lace cap. Meg. Who else could it be? She directs me back the way I came, across a small landing, to the bathroom. I go back to bed and sleep soundly.

In the morning over breakfast I tease Meg about her nocturnal attire. 'Lace cap? Virginal nightie? I had you down as the silk pyjamas type.'

Meg turns to her husband, busy spreading generous quantities of marmalade on his toast. 'Ken!' she scolds. 'For heaven's sake. What have I said to you about your mother? Wandering around the house at night, scaring the living daylights out of people. You have to speak to her!'

'Ken's mother?' I splutter, before Ken can answer. 'I didn't know she ...'

'No no, dear. She doesn't. She died five years ago. "Ninety-seven years young." That's how she described herself. I'm sorry about what happened last night. Must have given you an awful fright. Not the first time it's happened either. She's angry, you see. About the house. She wants it to be a family home again. Ken and I couldn't have children, something she never accepted. Went on at us about it as if we deliberately ... Well, never mind about that. Fact is, you're here, and there's a child running around, so she's making her presence felt.'

'I don't understand.' I look at Ken. He's a scientist. Surely he isn't buying into this?

He winks at me. 'I know,' he says. 'Mad. Stark staring. But then if you'd known my mother ...'

For much of the day I wonder if I shouldn't be getting myself and my daughter to the station and catching the next train back to London. But the day is so full of wonders, by the end of it I've decided the lady in the cap was a figment of my over-active imagination.

Ken parks the car in the driveway and walks on ahead of us, carrying the basket full of our beach-combing treasures. He pushes open the door – he prides himself on never having to lock it – and lets out a hoot of surprise. We catch up with him. What we see leaves me speechless; my daughter squeals with delight. Arranged on the lower steps of the central staircase facing the front door is a range of children's toys, the old-fashioned kind: a rocking horse; a musical box; a Punch and Judy theatre; a glass-eyed doll dressed in Victorian pantaloons; a large, one-eyed teddy bear; a doll's house; a Meccano set; a gaily coloured spinning top ... I don't remember who spoke first, but I can hear Meg's voice upbraiding her husband for the second time that day.

'You didn't speak to her, did you? And now look. What on earth are we meant to do? No one will ever want to visit us again ...'

Needless to say, this new mystery dominates the conversation for the rest of the evening. I venture to suggest that as the door was unlocked someone else could have put the toys there. Ken has a sister living nearby. Couldn't she, knowing there was a child staying, have brought the toys to the house? She'd not have needed a key to get in. Ken dismisses my explanation as even more preposterous than the idea of his dead mother carting toys down from the attic and arranging them on the stairs. By the end of the evening, having drunk two glasses of strong cider, I've decided we're all mad.

The teddy bear comes back with us to London. It's almost as big as my daughter. It's called Clifford, Ken's name for it when he was a boy.

A decade and a half later, learning of Meg's death close on the heels of Ken's, I discover that Trewinney is on the market. I drive down to Cornwall, determined to buy it. What was I thinking? 'Mad. Stark staring mad.' I can hear Ken's voice as I park my car in the muddy driveway bordered by wild, wind-pruned Cornish oaks. My own money has gone. There are debts. I walk towards the house I have re-imagined more than once in my fiction, stare through the window of its antiquated kitchen (the house is not just locked, most of its windows are boarded up), and spy the tea towel I used to dry the dishes. I'm sure it's the same one. Things changed very slowly if at all in this magical place.

I lean my head against the window frame, and weep.

**Return to Talland Bay**

To arrive here is to feel a falling away of fear.

I saw it this time in the moonlight first,
stood where black rock fell into the sea,
listening as the day's drowned whisper rose.

Christmas lights festooned the grey house on the cliff,
bats swooped in caves where ghostly miners trod,
dreams hung, bird-like, in the frost-bright air.

To be here is to know the wholeness of time –
Christ, the dark gods, rock, tin, and moon.

# Chapter Fifteen

Towards the end of the summer of 1970 we move from Marloes Road to South Hill Park Gardens in Belsize Park. It's something of a miracle, this shift from a shared flat in a down-at-heel Kensington street to a place of our own within coo-ee of Hampstead Heath. The workers of the miracle are my cousin Carolyn and her English husband Michael. Carolyn, a talented dancer, is the daughter of my mother's first cousin Kath, an Alley, like my mother. She and Michael have returned from the States where they spent a year, Michael teaching social work at the University of Wisconsin, Carolyn teaching dance. Now, some time later, having received an unexpected inheritance, they are the proud owners of a house large enough to accommodate two families. Would we like to rent, for mate's rates, the one-bedroom, self-contained flat on the top floor? Would we what!

We move in as summer is ending. I am by now six months pregnant. Despite ongoing morning sickness, I am over the moon at the prospect of having a second child. I practise saying the word 'children'. 'I have two children, a boy and a girl.' Or, 'I have two daughters, one's five, the other just a baby.' So great is my excitement I fail to notice that it is not shared.

A few weeks after we move, my mother-in-law arrives from New Zealand for an indefinite stay. Mike and Carolyn, having already extended our accommodation to include a bedroom on the floor below our flat, generously offer the room opposite for our long-term guest. Nain – Welsh for Grandma – with whom my daughter and I lodged prior to leaving New Zealand, will stay with us for the best part of a year. I am often grateful to her for her help, but it is not an easy visit.

Nain believes in witches. 'Most Welsh people do,' she tells me. It's early on in her stay. We've been sitting in not quite companionable silence waiting for *Coronation Street* – an essential part of her day, and the reason we've acquired a television set – to begin. 'There are white witches and black witches,' she goes on, warming to her theme. 'I'm a white witch, and I can tell you now, you are going to have a boy.'

I know better than to contradict her, so all I say is, 'I don't care what sex it is. So long as it has ten fingers and toes.'

'You want me to prove it's a boy?' she challenges.

I laugh. 'How are you supposed to do that?'

Her answer is to take out a cotton reel from the sewing basket at her feet, attach a piece of string to it and hold it over my pregnant belly. 'See?' she announces triumphantly. 'It swings to the left. That means it's a boy.'

A few weeks later she's proved right, but that doesn't persuade me to believe in witches. What I do believe in is the power my mother-in-law exercises over her immediate family which now, of course, includes me. Years later when she suffers a stroke, and my son (aged seven) and I fly out to New Zealand to take care of her, I became even more aware of this power. My marriage, unbeknownst to Nain or indeed anyone, is in trouble. Is this why I'm greeted coolly on arrival? Is she resentful that I'm the one who's flown across the world rather than her son? I tell myself it will get better. She's had a nasty fright. She's understandably on edge. But it gets worse. I cook the wrong food. I have the wrong friends. I should be earning a decent wage as a teacher, not wasting my time (she doesn't actually say this, but it's implied) writing novels. Worst of all, I'm a failure as a mother. 'My boys and I never had a blue day,' she claims, after watching me struggle through another decidedly blue day, negotiating with my strong-willed son.

As soon as Nain is able to take care of herself I pack my bags. We part – to, I suspect, mutual relief, on good terms. We never see each other again.

* * *

My son is born on November 29th. The hospital, like the school my daughter goes to, is a Hampstead village institution, but it is scheduled for closure (a decision that will subsequently be reversed). The day I'm admitted it's being run by a skeleton staff with only one qualified doctor in attendance. Consequently I am to be looked after by the midwife. This would not normally be a problem, but my baby is lying in the breach position, and the law in England is that a doctor must be present at a breach birth. Trouble is, the only available doctor has just finished a fourteen-hour shift, so the midwife – a worried-looking, middle-aged Ghanaian lady – decides that rather than wake the exhausted man, she will try to move the baby so he or she is facing the right way. After she's made several painful attempts to do this, I beg her to stop. I've already told her my first baby was a footling breach and the birth went ahead without a hitch, but she doesn't seem to understand what I'm saying.

Hours pass: a day and most of a night. The baby is now lying sideways, and no matter how many times the midwife tries to move my reluctant son or daughter, nothing happens. Bruce visits but doesn't stay. Then Vernon arrives, takes stock of the situation and stays. The nurses assume he's the father and address him as such. I tell him not to correct them in case they ask him to leave. Vernon fetches me juice and rubs my aching back. Best of all, he tells me the words I need to hear – that it will be all right, it will be over soon.

Eventually Bruce returns and Vernon leaves.

What follows is best left unrecorded. I am not the first woman, nor will I be the last, to learn a hard truth about the father of her child at the time of giving birth. Recently I read Kate Grenville's brilliant memoir of her mother, *One Life*. Speaking in her mother's voice, Kate describes the night her son was born. The pains start on Christmas Day. The hospital is only a few blocks away, so Nance and her husband Ken set out to walk the short distance from their home. But they are no sooner out the door than the contractions become really strong, obliging Nance to 'stop and lean against someone's fence' until they pass. Ken turns his back on her. This is the moment when Nance realises her husband doesn't love her. 'He was embarrassed, she understood that … frightened … But she was frightened too … What sort of person would turn away at such a time?'

That my son and I survive is nothing short of a miracle. That the marriage survives for another twelve years has nothing to do with miracles and everything to do with my determination never to be divorced again. The poems I wrote during my extended stay in hospital are lost, but nothing is forgotten.

* * *

The day I return with my two-and-a-half-week-old baby to the flat in South Hill Park Gardens, there is snow on the ground and trouble in the body politic. Since June and the defeat of Harold Wilson's Labour government, the Conservatives, under Edward Heath, have been in power. But hopes that the new government might succeed, where Labour had failed, to curb the unrest in the country have been dashed. The car industry is in trouble. The government has had to step in to save Rolls Royce. Soon it will have to do the same for British Leyland. Similarly with the coal industry: the miners are demanding wage increases which the government insists it cannot pay. Then the dockers go on strike and a state of emergency is declared. But there is worse to come. In Derry, Northern Ireland, the arrest of the Republican Ulster MP, Bernadette Devlin, leads to rioting, a situation inflamed by the demented oratory of the newly elected MP for North Antrim, the Reverend Ian Paisley. In July British troops engage in a pitched battle with the IRA on the streets of Belfast. Three civilians are killed.

This is the world I am returning to from the no-man's land of sickness. I look at my son, frail in my arms, and I think of the words I'd read in hospital: 'Here is the world. Beautiful and terrible things will happen. Don't be afraid.' I couldn't have said then who wrote those words, but I know now that the author was the American theologian, Frederick Buechner. Discovering his lines, when looking for something else, jolted me back to that time when the world did indeed seem uniquely beautiful (my son) and terrible (civil war in Ireland; social unrest in England). I don't remember being afraid. What I remember is being intensely aware of everything around me.

I climb the stairs to our flat, embrace my mother-in-law and head out again to fetch my daughter from school, leaving the baby with his grandmother. As a treat to compensate for my long absence and the potentially disturbing presence in her life of a baby brother, I take my daughter out for a special tea. When it's time to go home, we step outside and head for the car. Suddenly, without warning, all the lights go out, not just in the street but all over Hampstead. It's as if we've had hoods thrown over our faces. There are voices everywhere, shouting, screaming, crying. Somehow I grope my way to the car and turn on the lights. Others have done the same. But the beams scarcely penetrate the suffocating darkness. I start to drive, crawling out of the parking place, tooting the horn. All I can see is the few inches of road in front of me. I don't even know if I'm facing in the right direction. But I have to keep moving. My son is due his next feed.

An hour and a quarter later, having covered a distance of less than two miles, I reach home. The lights are still not on but people have come out of their houses with torches and candles, making navigation possible. I take the stairs two at a time. I can hear my son crying.

That blackout marked the beginning of a crisis that would last almost the entire decade. Ahead of us were petrol rationing, more blackouts and a period of electricity cuts that came to be known as the 'three-day week'. Ahead for me was a new kind of family life, a move out of London, the joys and tribulations of writing, and the creation of a home – a word I now begin to use for the first time since childhood.

# Chapter Sixteen

Last night I dreamed I was sitting in front of a very dark cake – so dark it was almost black. As I carefully cut a slice, I realised the cake was Time. There had been no invitation to eat, so this wasn't an Alice in Wonderland dream. But neither had there been there a warning *not* to eat. So I took a bite. The taste was not unpleasant, but it *was* bitter. I looked around for something to go with it – cream or yoghurt – but the only thing on the table was the cake and the knife to slice it. Clearly I would have to eat it plain or not at all.

Is writing a memoir a way of eating Time? It's certainly a way of recovering it, though what I'm discovering as I re-imagine events, some of which seem to have happened only yesterday, is that many of the things I think I've remembered turn out, on closer inspection (and consultation with others who were there) to have happened differently, in another place, at another time. So what was the dream telling me? That I should be careful what I eat? That Time Remembered can leave a bitter taste?

* * *

**Night Thoughts**

Night clings to the shuddering trees.
Light is rubbed out of the sky.
I stare at the shape of the house next to mine.
It drops into darkness, dead as a stone.

If I close my eyes I can see the stars,
cloud-encrusted, partly bright. Will they shine,
do you think, on my night-stained house,
densely bricked against the wind?

I crouch by the window.
The dead house stares.
No stars burn the silence.
Light disappears.

I remember exactly where I was sitting when I wrote that poem: by the window of our top-floor Hampstead flat looking down on the tiny, crescent-shaped garden, the lights of the other houses in the street transforming the bare-branched plane trees into thin-fingered ghosts. I sound depressed, but that's not what I remember. I believe now that I was gradually distancing myself from the dream of intimacy and replacing it with a different dream, one in which the only person who could let me down was myself. I wrote poems. I'd written two as yet unpublished novels. Was I already a writer? It would be several years before I called myself that, but the words were there now, shaping themselves into stories, beating a tattoo in my head as I went about my daily, child-centred life.

* * *

'As an imaginative writer my only capital is my own life.' The words are Ted Hughes', from his essay *Poetry in the Making*, but what he is saying is true, at some level, of every fiction writer. So I go back to the beginning, to *No Daffodils for Mrs Browning*, to ask myself the question that has been bugging me ever since I started writing memoir. What *is* the relationship between the lived life and fiction? The girl/woman at the centre of *No Daffodils* lives in 1950s Dunedin, the same world I lived in. Her name is Geraldine McKenzie, a Scottish name, like mine. Her father dies when she is fourteen. So did mine. Her mother is mentally unstable. So was mine. She has an older brother. So did I. They are both adopted. So were we. What I don't recognise is the girl herself. Is that passivity mine? Is that willingness to play the martyr mine? I look at this early, failed novel with its obvious flaws – wonky chronology, inconsistencies, overwriting – and I have to acknowledge that right from the start I was drawing on the 'capital' of my own life. Even when I was writing about John Donne, or telling a story based on Scottish emigration to Otago, I was drawing on that capital. Those novels may seem to belong to another universe from the one I inhabited at the time of writing, but the links are there: the search for love; for (overused word) authenticity; for a place to call home; for God. In *Catch a Falling Star* there's even a link I could not possibly have foreseen in Donne's agonised conversion from Catholicism to Anglicanism and my own journey the other way, from the Protestantism of my childhood to the Catholicism of Pope Francis.

*No Daffodils* fails as a psychological thriller. Too much is given away too soon. But what I see now is that in its search for motive, for an explanation for human behaviour, I was laying down a blueprint for everything that would follow. In that first unsuccessful drawing on the 'capital' of my life, I had found my way to tell stories.

* * *

We stay in South Hill Park Gardens for just under two years. In many ways it's a rich and exciting time. Bruce is the gregarious type. He likes to entertain the people he's working with, the more famous the better. Friendships are made, some of which last; others, despite all the hugging and flirting, the easy endearments – I've never been able to shake the habit, acquired during this time, of calling people 'love' – vanish into the theatrical ether. A procession of actors, writers, directors and musicians cross our threshold, but it's not these faces that are vivid to me now, but two people who had nothing to do with the arts. One is a Pakistani doctor, father of a school friend of my daughter's, the other a Kiwi woman of my own age who turns up on my doorstep one winter's morning and stays four months.

* * *

The first time we visit Salem and his English wife, Loretta, I feel as if I've been transported to a grown-up version of Santa's magic grotto. I am literally dazzled by gold! It's everywhere – in the curtains, the carpets, on the walls, in the sari that blonde-haired Loretta is wearing, in the beads around her neck and wrists, in Salem's teeth ... There are ornaments, some lining shelves, others free-standing on the floor, that are all gold. I look down at my flared trousers and ethnic blouse, and stifle the urge to run.

But Salem could not be more welcoming. Whiskeys are poured (Salem is a Muslim but alcohol restrictions clearly don't apply); delicious, highly perfumed food is served, one dish following another as if this were an official feast, not just a 'casual' dinner; stories are told; jokes are made. Salem tells us he is the official doctor for the MCC (Marylebone Cricket Club). He pulls back one of the heavy gold curtains to show us the lights of the cricket ground on the other side of the street. I wonder if the MCC is paying for this luxurious apartment, but can't, of course, put the thought into words.

By the end of the evening we are friends.

The night they come to have dinner with us in South Hill Park Gardens, I decide to wear the long muumuu dress I have just bought from Marks and Spencer's. A mistake. Loretta arrives wearing a cream trouser suit with bright gold earrings and sexy sandals. I feel a frump. I've laboured over the meal – chestnut soup followed by beef stroganoff – which I'd hoped would have its own unique flavours, just as Loretta's had. The first course goes off without a hitch, but the stroganoff creates a hideously embarrassing moment when Salem struggles to chew on the bouquet-garni sachet I have neglected to remove. Everyone but me finds this funny. More wine is poured and the evening, the first of many, proceeds merrily.

Over the next few years there are regular visits to and from Salem and his family. They come to stay with us after we move to the Cotswolds. We have dinner with them when we come to London. Then, without explanation, they disappear. I assume they have gone back to Pakistan, but with no address other than the house opposite the famous cricket ground, I have no way of tracking them down. Thinking of them now, wondering what might have happened to them during Pakistan's many coups, I find myself remembering a meeting with Salem's father, a humble GP from Peshawar. While still living in Hampstead we were invited to dinner to meet him. His shabby brown suit and gentle courtesy were in marked contrast to the flamboyant manners and appearance of his son. He and I fell into a conversation about life in London. 'Salem drives a Rolls Royce,' the old man said, a puzzled smile on his face. 'Why such a grand car? In London there are many cars. But his is the best, yes? The most expensive.'

'Not really,' I answered. 'There are many people in London who want you to know how rich they are. At least Salem only has one car. In Bishops Avenue there's a man, a sheikh, who owns a whole fleet of Rolls Royces.'

'If my son were living in Peshawar he would ride the biggest elephant,' he said, his smile sad now. 'That is who he is.'

I don't like not knowing what has happened to people I have grown close to. Over the years, whenever Pakistan is in the news (when is it not?), I find myself scanning the names of that troubled country's movers and shakers for mention of Salem. But I have never found him.

* * *

Laura. It's not her real name. I wonder if it's the name I gave her in the play, *No Fixed Address*, which I wrote after we'd moved to the Cotswolds – the play I was looking for when I found *No Daffodils*. I deplore this tendency to lose things that are important to me. Thanks to my mother's strict upbringing – she used to boast she was training me as she had once trained probationer nurses – I'm a highly organised person domestically. But in my writing life I seem to sink back into some kind of primeval chaos. My writing is illegible even to me, after a day or two. I make notes, which I then lose. Trying to find the shape of a story, I go off at so many tangents I end up with six possible stories, which is the same as saying I end up with none.

But though I've lost the script of *No Fixed Address*, and can't remember the names I gave my characters, I do remember the story. It was my first original play for the BBC. Prior to that I'd done only adaptations. I'd worked with Rosamond Lehmann, still beautiful in her eighties, on four of her novels – *The Weather in the Streets*, *Invitation to the Waltz*, *Dusty Answer* and *The Echoing Grove*. Later I would go on to adapt novels by Elizabeth Taylor, Martin Boyd and John Galsworthy, but working with Rosamond and BBC producer Jane Morgan (who became a close friend) was not just the start of it all, it was the highlight. Had Laura not come into my life, it's possible I would have gone on doing adaptations, leaving original work for novels and short stories. I can think of no greater pleasure than immersing myself in the worlds of writers I admire. Laura changed all that. I *had* to tell her story, which of course was also my story, and the story of my family. It was the only way I could come to terms with the whirlpool of emotions she unleashed. Not to mention the guilt I felt about abandoning her (as I did eventually), and my complex feelings towards her as the mother of my much-loved god-daughter. It never occurred to me to write the story as a novel. The voices in my head were too insistent for that.

Laura and I had been friends in Auckland, though I wouldn't have described us as close. After I left the country we lost touch. Laura was married to M, a man I'd known since I was a student and was close to. They had a daughter, the same age as my daughter. When I was told by a mutual friend that Laura had abandoned both her marriage and her child, my initial reaction was disbelief. Laura was one of the women who, during my furtive, solo-mother days, shared with me her restlessness and dissatisfaction, but I'd never imagined her walking out on her child. She was taking a break, that's all.

Now here she was, two years later, standing on my doorstep looking like a famine victim. I knew she'd gone to India. I presumed she, like so many others at the time, had gone in search of 'enlightenment', and that when she found it she'd go home again. Unfortunately, enlightenment eluded her. What she found instead was drugs and death. The man she was travelling with died of an overdose, leaving her with no money and no means of support. So she turned to the one person she knew would help her – her ex-husband. I never did ask why the airline ticket M sent her was to England and not New Zealand. Perhaps I was afraid to hear the answer.

'How did you know where I live?' I say, as I lead the skeletal figure, whose identity I am still trying to come to terms with, up the stairs to our flat.

'M gave me your address,' she answers. 'I didn't know anyone else.' She flashes me a heart-breaker of a smile. 'Hope you don't mind.'

For the next four months Laura will be as much a part of my life as my two children. I don't need to be told what her problem is. The very first night I find her in the bathroom, huddled on the floor with her back to the bath, shaking like a dog after a swim. I make her a hot drink and get her back to bed. Next morning I consult my cousin Michael. As a man trained in social work he's used to dealing with addicts. He'll know what to do. The following day I take Laura to the doctor Michael has recommended. He prescribes methadone. I tell myself this will be the end of the problem, but I'm wrong. The night shakes go on, as do the alarming mood swings. Laura offers to babysit for us (my son is only a few weeks old), but I worry she won't be able to cope.

I do very little writing during this time. It's as if I have been asked to take care of a third child. Laura, on a good day, is enchanting company. Friends who come to our house are fascinated by her. She tells them the story of her life with admirable restraint and self-mockery. Vernon, the man who holds my career as well as my husband's in his hands, falls in love with her. Does this mean he isn't really gay? I even wonder if my husband is a little in love with her as well. The bad days, which outnumber the good, almost always happen when he's away.

Eventually I give in and agree to let Laura babysit. I've not been out socially for weeks. I want to go somewhere for a quiet dinner but we've been invited to a party, and parties, in my husband's world, invariably trump intimate dinners.

The evening is a disaster. Shortly after arriving at our friend's house, an hour's drive away, there's a phone call summoning us back home. It's not from Laura, it's from Michael. I was right. Laura couldn't cope.

Next morning, over a tense breakfast, I stammer out the words I've made up my mind to say. 'Laura ... I'm sorry ... if this was our place ... but it's not. I think you should find somewhere else to stay.'

Laura frowns, as if doubting what she's heard, then her eyes widen in shock. 'You're throwing me out –'

'No! It's just –'

'Where do you expect me to go? A hotel? I don't have any money.'

'I know, and I'll help you of course, but –'

'I don't know anyone in London. You're the only person –'

'Michael knows someone ... a job ... live in ... I've been meaning to talk to you about it.'

'So you've been planning this all along. You and Michael.'

'No ... I –'

'You've never been any good at lying,' she says.

Helping her pack her meagre belongings, driving her round to her new home (my memory is that it was not far), I feel as if I'm driving a reluctant novice to a nunnery. Three days later, she's back on our doorstep. I have no memory now of what went wrong for her, only of how I felt leading her up the stairs for the second time.

For a few weeks things go well. Laura's night sweats stopped some time ago. She no longer looks like a skeleton. I plan small excursions: coffee in Belsize Village; walks on the Heath; window shopping in Hampstead. Most of Laura's clothes are floaty Indian garments made of cotton and silk, but this is winter, so she has to borrow jerseys and coats to keep warm. We bemoan our mutual lack of funds. Window shopping is no substitute for the real thing. Not that Laura ever looks poverty stricken. Even wearing jerseys two sizes too big for her, she looks glamorous. I feel shabby alongside her. I smell of baby sick. I observe with astonishment, and more than a twinge of jealousy, her growing friendship with Vernon. Isn't he supposed to be *my* friend? Watching the two of them from the upstairs window, walking hand in hand down the hill on their way to a first night, I experience a suffocating wave of self-pity. In the past Vernon would have taken me.

In the end it's Michael who forces the issue. He and Carolyn want their spare room back. I suspect he is more concerned about me than he is about his proprietary rights, but whatever his motivation, the die is cast. There is now nowhere for Laura to sleep. She has to go.

It will be more than a decade before I see her again. Miraculously we are able to be friends. She has reconnected with her daughter and made dramatic changes to her life. Married with two more children, she is still glamorous, still able to turn heads; still, in ways that move me despite our history, a lost soul.

*No Fixed Address* is broadcast in 1983. It stars Lisa Harrow, Barbara Ewing and James Laurenson, three Kiwi actors who already have impressive careers. I can't deny that the play is autobiographical, but it also owes something to Sartre's *Huis Clos (No Exit)*, a play I studied at university. 'Hell is other people,' says Sartre's Joseph. I don't agree with that statement, but for those four fraught months, living in close quarters with a woman for whom the normal rules didn't apply, there were moments when I knew what he meant.

Looking back on *No Fixed Address* and the experience that inspired it, I see Laura as both unique and typical. She was adrift in a world of disappearing values and shifting allegiances. Compared to her, I was lucky. I had children to anchor me. But she had abandoned her child and with it – despite the message of Doris Lessing, who famously left her two oldest children behind when she fled Rhodesia – her chance of finding true freedom. That the play was produced in both England and New Zealand seems to me now to prove that what was going on in individual lives in 1970s England was mirrored throughout the Western world. Thanks to the revolution in communication, no corner of the globe would ever again be safe from the intrusion of the camera and the satellite.

Laura had left New Zealand in the grip of an idea that had its origins in the hippy movement of the 1960s. In retreat from that idea, she would eventually return to New Zealand, but she wouldn't stay. A new phase of human history – globalisation, with its collapsing of national and personal identities – had begun.

# Chapter Seventeen

A lot has been written about the 1970s. Described by novelist Tom Wolfe in an essay published in 1976 as the 'Me Decade', it has been blamed by many writers of both fiction and non-fiction for most if not all the ills that attend us in this second decade of the twenty-first century. The growing gap between rich and poor, the spread of terrorism, the bloody progress of ISIS, the threat to the future of the planet, the Brexit vote and the rise of Donald Trump have all been traced back to the decade which ended with the election of Margaret Thatcher as British prime minister, closely followed by Ronald Reagan's victory in the US. From this point on, neo-liberalism would dominate the politics of the West. The compassionate economics of John Maynard Keynes, which had informed governments throughout the 'free world' since the war, were consigned to history. 'There is no society,' Thatcher famously declared, as she set about making sure her assertion became fact.

I don't necessarily disagree with this analysis, but my memories of this time are not of laissez faire acceptance, which you might expect from a self-absorbed generation, but of passionate resistance to what was happening in the political and economic arenas. Maybe this is me 'taking control' of memory, the inevitable consequence, in the view of philosopher and critic Walter Benjamin, of writing about the past. 'To articulate what is past does not mean to recognise *how it really was*,' he wrote. 'It means to take control of memory …' If that *is* what I'm doing – rearranging things to make the past more palatable – I can only say in my defence that that is not what I *feel* I'm doing. We were a protesting generation. We may have lost our best leaders to assassinations – John and Bobby Kennedy, Martin Luther King – but we hadn't given up on the values they represented. The Vietnam War was still raging. Nuclear weapons were proliferating around the world. Israel, following its victory in the 1967 Six Day War, was busy asserting its right to dominate Palestine. There was plenty to protest about.

So I take my children on CND marches in London and to demonstration days at Greenham Common, home to the notorious Cruise missiles. I join the Labour Party, then help establish a branch in the Cotswold village we move to early in 1972. I vote against the EEC (as it was called then) in the 1975 referendum, not because I'm a Kiwi but because I want Britain to be involved in a trading partnership with the Commonwealth. Later, in the 1980s, I will send money to help the coalminers in their long, doomed dispute with Thatcher's government, and make regular (illegal) payments to the families of ANC men and women imprisoned by the apartheid government of South Africa. I adopt a Kenyan boy as part of a scheme to educate poor African children. I join others from my village and travel to Upper Heyford, where the American Air Force is based, to protest, along with many Tories, the 1986 bombing of Libya. I have a vivid memory of standing next to a middle-aged lady with blue-rinsed hair, a proud Tory 'of the old-fashioned kind' (her description), haranguing a seven-foot black Texan soldier on the other side of the high wire fence separating the American base from the protesters: 'Now look here, my good man, I don't come into your country and fly planes from your airfields to bomb places I've hardly even heard of. So please would you go back to your country, which I'm told is a very fine place to live, and stop flying those frightful planes of yours over our farms and fields in the middle of the night. Really! Such inconsideration. You should be ashamed of yourself!'

Was all that protesting in vain? It's easy to think so when you look at the record. The 1973 American-backed military coup in Chile, which replaced the socialist government of Salvador Allende with the neo-liberal, crypto-fascist regime of Augusto Pinochet, was only one in a number of US interventions in South American politics culminating, the following decade, in the Iran/Contra arms for hostages scandal that nearly brought down the Reagan government. President Nixon's resignation in 1974 following the Watergate scandal may look now like a sign of things to come – the gradual erosion of trust in democratically elected leaders – but we saw it as a victory. The Senate hearings, aired on British television at 11 o'clock every night, were as addictive as soap opera. The papers were full of it; conversations were dominated by it; people of all persuasions were united in their belief that it could never happen in England.

So do we blame the 'Me Decade' for the fact that thirty-five years later we find ourselves in a world of selfies and Facebook friendships, where mass killings by individuals who see no place for themselves in our degraded society occur with terrifying regularity? 'Greed is Good', the mantra of the Reagan–Thatcher years, had, and has, many adherents. But not everyone bought into it, and not everyone has been silenced.

* * *

Trawling through memory, looking for clues as to why things happened, is not an exercise in futility, as some might claim, but part of living what Socrates called the 'examined life', the only life, he insisted, that's worth living. The trouble is, the deeper you journey into the past, the more the picture changes. Start from a different place and a new set of memories will arrive, giving a whole new slant to the story you're telling. So I go back again to the experts, pondering their verdict that our current woes were seeded in the ideas being promulgated during the 60s and 70s, and I'm at a loss to explain why it didn't seem at the time as if the death knell of decent liberal democracy was being sounded, but rather that barriers were being knocked down, and things hitherto regarded as impossible were suddenly, miraculously, within reach.

For my own part I can't help wondering if I would ever have been published had I landed on English shores a decade earlier or, for that matter, two decades later. The old bastions of the cultural status quo – publishing, the theatre, the BBC – were being besieged by the brave new worlds of film (freed from the censorship of Hollywood) and television. Barriers based on class and education, and the sound you made when you opened your mouth, were being shattered in plays written by 'angry young men' (and women) and films and television made by such socially conscious directors as Ken Loach. His docu-drama *Cathy Come Home*, which I saw again recently, packs as powerful a punch today as it did when it was first aired to a shocked nation in 1966. So a young woman who is constantly mistaken for a Rhodesian, who went to school 12,000 miles away, and who knows no one in the publishing world is, thanks to the brave people who knocked down those barriers, taken seriously as a writer. I suspect it would not have happened at any other time.

Shortly after *Catch a Falling Star* is published (to this day, I regret not calling it *The Mandrake Root*, the words in the next line of Donne's poem), I'm taken on by up-and-coming literary agent Deborah Rogers. Vernon, having acknowledged that as a theatrical agent he doesn't have the contacts of other exclusively literary agents, is generous about the move. Almost overnight I find myself in the same stable as Ian McEwan, Shena Mackay (who some years later will become a close friend) and Salman Rushdie. Deborah's nose for new talent and for stories that challenged the existing order will take her to the very top of her profession. She takes my second novel, *The Broken Tree*, about Scottish emigration to Otago, to Hutchinson. Blond & Briggs is no longer in existence. I used to joke that I had personally bankrupted them – *Catch a Falling Star* was one of the last novels they published – but in fact *Catch* did reasonably well, garnering decent reviews in both the UK and Commonwealth press.

But I would have left Blond & Briggs anyway. Post-publication, Anthony and I were at loggerheads. His view of my writing future was very different from my own.

'Shelley,' he announced, over another extravagant lunch. 'That's the guy you should be thinking about. Only this time let's have everything in there. The ménage à trois, the free love, the incest, the atheism ...'

I grinned at him. I knew what he was thinking. My take on John Donne had never been racy enough for him. 'You don't think Donne slept with boys?' he'd challenged when I presented the manuscript to him. 'Come on. He was randy as a trout. Why isn't there some gay sex in here?' Shelley, I realised, as I listened to Anthony's description of the novel he was so sure I was going to write, was my chance to redeem myself for the gaps in my John Donne story.

Telling him no wasn't easy. I knew how lucky I was to have a publisher of his standing on my side. So I told him it wasn't so much that I didn't want to write about Shelley, I didn't want to write historical fiction at all. I'd only written about Donne because I was fascinated by him. More than a little in love with him too, despite his being dead 400 years. But I had none of those feelings for Shelley, and no desire at all (this I didn't say) to write another novel about a dead poet.

So I wrote *The Broken Tree*, a novel that owes a large debt to the stories my adoptive father told me. It was published in 1981. It's set in the nineteenth century, so it would seem I was throwing in my lot with historical fiction after all. But the truth is, I don't choose the time frame of the stories I write – they choose me. A character, an event, an atmosphere, even a line of dialogue will take root in my mind, and slowly, as this 'cerebral pregnancy' develops, other things will adhere to that tiny seed and a story will evolve. The three novels I wrote after *The Broken Tree* are all set in the twentieth century, as are all but one of the original plays I wrote for the BBC. But I confess I'm unable to write up-to-the minute contemporary fiction, as the incomparable Margaret Atwood or New Zealand's Charlotte Grimshaw do so brilliantly. I have huge admiration for their ability to find what is both universal and strange in contemporary life, but I seem to need Kierkegaard's distance: life, which must be lived forwards, can 'only be understood backwards ...'

*The Broken Tree* is an emigration story centred on the Scottish diaspora that followed the notorious Highland Clearances. Steeped in Presbyterianism, it contains just a hint of Catholic 'otherness'. Much has been said about the prescient nature of writing, the way in which writers anticipate events that subsequently come to pass. George Orwell's *Nineteen Eighty-four* or H.G. Wells' *Brave New World* may have seemed shocking when first published, but the element of shock disappeared once the world caught up with their visions of the future. What is harder to explain is when a writer describes something in her fiction which then becomes a reality in her life. This has happened to me twice. The first time was in *The Broken Tree*, when I signalled my attraction to the 'other' world of Catholicism. Had anyone told me that three decades later I would abandon my lifelong Protestantism in favour of the Church of Pope Francis, I would have reacted with disbelief. The second time was when, some years after the publication of my 1995 novel *River Lines*, a story with an adoption at its heart, I discovered that the circumstances of my own adoption were similar in almost every aspect to the ones I had imagined.

I love coincidences. They are one of fiction's most useful – and used – tools, the means by which a pattern can be shaped out of seemingly random events. In some stories they are not just tools, they are the place where meaning resides. So the coincidence of my imagining in my fiction something which later turns out to be broadly true in my own life is not really so remarkable. There are things we know at an unconscious level that we are quite unable, consciously, to put into words. We are shadowed by our pasts, remembered and forgotten, just as we are shadowed by all the people we have come into contact with. Sitting in front of my computer, typing out these words, I like to think I am accompanied by all the people I know and have known, and all the people I love and have loved, whose voices I hear as echoes, whose breath I feel on my cheek.

*The Broken Tree* goes on to sell in the United States under a different title. When I see the American version, with its lurid cover and hideous title – *The Burning Dawn* – I burst into tears. From that day on I make sure I have veto rights over both title changes and choice of cover. Had I been less in awe of Anthony Blond I would have protested his choice of cover for *Catch a Falling Star*. I hated it!

The novel sells well. Hutchinson want me to write another novel set in the nineteenth century: emigration stories are easy to sell in the States. I'd be foolish not to build on my success. The conversation I have with my editor about this is easier (and more sober) than my encounters with Anthony, but my answer is still no. I have another tale to tell, one set in the twentieth century. The story of a pacifist in World War II has been taking shape in my mind ever since John and Shirley shared their wartime experiences with me. Could I have been a pacifist? That's the question I have been asking myself. Now, having decided to try to answer this question in the only way I know – by writing a novel – I set out to read everything I can about the war and New Zealand's treatment of its conscientious objectors. As I pore over records of conscription and war resistance, pondering the attitudes of my fellow New Zealanders to the men and women who refused to have anything to do with war, other questions, equally difficult to answer, take shape in my mind. Does war ever solve anything? Where does the greatest courage lie – in resisting war, or in accepting it as inevitable and donning a uniform?

By the time I'm ready to write the book I have a new publisher, Secker & Warburg, and a new editor, Peter Grose. It's Peter who persuades me that I should also write about a soldier, balancing his experience with the experiences of my conscientious objector. So I head to the London Library and the library at New Zealand House and get out everything I can find on the New Zealand Expeditionary Forces fighting in North Africa and Greece. I spend whole days in the Imperial War Museum looking at unedited footage of the battles for Greece and Crete. What happens to me during this period of research (I have been paid a handsome advance) is that I fall in love. Not with my character this time but with a country – Greece.

I visit Greece in the spring of 1981. I climb Mount Hymettus on the outskirts of Athens where the New Zealanders had their camp. With a young family waiting for me back in England I don't have time to get to the places in the north where the Kiwis fought and died, but I do have time to get to Crete, where a large part of my story is set. So I board the ferry at Piraeus, crossing the same waters the soldiers crossed, seeing the same islands spread, like indolent sunbathers, across the 'wine-dark' sea.

Crete is a revelation. I feel its difference from Greece long before I'm told by the proudest people on Earth that they are not Greek, they are Cretan. On this legendary island every citizen has a story to tell, usually one involving suicidal deeds of heroism against either the Ottomans or the Germans. I'm taken to three different caves and told, on oath, that this is the cave where 'my uncle' or 'my cousin' or, in one case, 'my father' helped Patrick Leigh Fermor and his band of Allied and Greek resistance fighters hide the captured German general, Heinrich Kreipe, a feat celebrated in the film *Ill Met by Moonlight*. Despite an almost total language barrier, I'm interviewed in the local paper. Soon people are coming up to me in the street, anxious to tell me their stories. I go to the inland village of Galatos to see the memorial to the soldiers of the Māori Battalion who died defending it. I stand in front of that dazzling white monument, Māori names coupled with Cretan names, the fern coupled with the laurel branch, and tears pour down my face.

A lifetime fascination is born. *Love and War* is published in 1982, but I can't leave the island alone. I play around with an idea for a film about the re-capture of Galatos, a victory in the midst of defeat that is celebrated every year, both in New Zealand and on Crete, on the anniversary of the battle. On a trip back to New Zealand I talk to film makers about the story. Interest is sparked. I'm encouraged. But nothing happens. This, I will learn in subsequent encounters with the film industry, is par for the course. The difficulties involved in getting a film made are biblical: it's like trying to get a camel through the eye of a needle.

I write other novels, other scripts, but Crete is still there, hovering in the wings, demanding to be centre stage again. In 2011 I write a play for Radio New Zealand called *The Cave of Winds*, set in a cave in the mountains of Crete just like the ones I visited. I had by this time read dozens of accounts of soldiers left behind in the chaos of evacuation following the German invasion. In my play I have a wounded Pākehā officer holed up in a cave with a Māori private from his platoon. So the play is as much about their relationship as it is about Crete and the war. *The Cave of Winds* wins Best Spoken Feature in the 2012 New Zealand Media Awards, but I'm still not done. In the wake of discovering that my birth mother's brother died on Crete ('missing presumed dead'), I adapt the play for the stage. The breath on my cheek as I write is my uncle's. His photo – he is handsome in his uniform – smiles back at me. What happened to him? Why was he not found? Did the Cretans shelter him as they sheltered so many Kiwis? Did he die alone? Was he in pain? Scared? Lonely? He is there, somewhere, on that island of heroes. I need to go back and find him.

*Love and War* will prove to be my most commercially successful novel. A paperback edition is published by Futura. Then in 1992 the novel is republished in the Vintage series by Random House New Zealand. The film rights sell three times, earning me enough, with the royalties from *The Broken Tree*, to pay the bills for several years. Disappointingly, it doesn't sell in the States. 'You needed to have a Yankee soldier in there somewhere,' Peter Grose tells me. I'll hear the same words when a film script is being written for producer John Barnett in New Zealand. Keith Aberdein is the writer. 'Going to take some liberties with your story,' he warns. 'If we want American money there's got to be American action. I'm thinking of the Manners Street Battle.' (I'd never heard of it). 'Should be able to get our hands on some good footage. My idea is to have a Yank stationed at Mackays Crossing who falls in love with a Māori girl from the farm. Sort of a sub-plot...'

The film never happens (why did I ever think it would?), though it goes a long way down the track. I'm disappointed, but I can't help wondering now if I'd have recognised my story.

# Chapter Eighteen

That we are able, in 1972, to buy a house in the Cotswolds is something of a miracle (I'm aware I've been over-using this word). It's not as if we have any money of our own. Anything that goes into our account invariably goes out the same day. But when Michael comes to tell me he and Carolyn are hoping to start a family, I know our days in leafy Hampstead are numbered. Sooner rather than later we're going to have to find a place of our own.

The idea of moving does not go down well with Bruce. We have been paying well below the market rent for a flat in one of the most desirable parts of London. Where are we supposed to go? I suggest we move out of the city – better for the children. But this idea meets with even more resistance. I don't have an answer, or even an argument, but I do have a vision. It's arrived as suddenly and unexpectedly as Michael's announcement, but now it's there I can't escape it. I want my children to experience the same freedom I experienced growing up in the safety of a small, tight-knit community. I *want* to move out of London.

I write to the trustee of my father's estate. Is there any chance money could be made available for me to buy a flat or a house outside London? The answer is not the one I'd hoped for, but it's hardly a surprise: 'Funds can only be released with your mother's permission. I will talk to her, but I have to warn you she is unlikely to agree.'

I say nothing to anyone about this, but I don't give up. I'm an optimist! 'It might help,' the trustee writes in a subsequent letter, 'if you had a specific property in mind.'

So I start looking. Surreptitiously. I scan newspapers, talk to friends living in a village in Buckinghamshire, sound out others living within a hundred-mile radius of London. My secret mission pays off. A friend, met through my son's playgroup, tells me her mother-in-law has bought a property in the Cotswolds and is anxious to sell the last remaining part of it to someone she knows. The property – an extended farmhouse dating back to the sixteenth century – is in a village called Ascott-under-Wychwood. It has a name – The Long House. But it's no longer a single dwelling. It's been converted into three homes. Phoebe, my friend's mother-in-law, an artist specialising in screen printing, lives in what was once the barn. Friends of hers (soon to be friends of ours) live in the former storage area at the other end. Would I be interested in looking at the main part of the building, the actual farmhouse? It comes with a coach house and stable, a paved courtyard and a walled garden with fruit trees. The pictures that form in my mind as I absorb this information merge into a bizarre collage of Englishness and New Zealandness. I see a typical English 'cottage' with roses trailing over the front door, surrounded by paddocks where a horse – our horse – prances and gallops while a dog – our dog – yaps excitedly at my heels.

But I'm still meeting with strong resistance to the idea of moving away from London. So I hold out a carrot – the prospect of money for this particular house arriving from New Zealand. It works. A day trip is planned. Just to have a look.

We set out on a chilly Saturday, driving through the city's congested streets till we hit the new motorway linking London with Oxford. I've been to the Cotswolds only once before, and though I found its villages, woods and rivers beautiful I never felt, as I had in Cornwall, an irresistible pull to come back. Yet here I am, skirting the dreaming spires of Oxford, heading for a village I've all but persuaded myself will soon be our home. As we glide down the hill into Ascott-under-Wychwood I turn to the children and say, 'Which house shall we have? They all look nice, don't you think?'

And they do. Only in Italy do you find stone as beautiful as the soft golden stone of the Cotswolds. In this unremarkable village, home to just over 400 people, almost all the cottages are built of it. No one set out to create beauty, but beauty is what's happened. I feel Bruce's resistance crumbling. The ease and speed of our journey have helped, but what helps more is the discovery that there is a regular fast train service from nearby Charlbury. By the time we have located the house, I have the scent of victory in my nostrils.

We park the car, and there it is, an eighteenth-century farmhouse – as it turns out, all that remains from Tudor times are two blackened beams – with an espaliered pear tree trailing across the wall to the left of the front door, and pale-blue wisteria lacing its way across the wall to the right. I had imagined roses, but this is better. I stand on the pavement, taking it all in. It's so quiet. The only sounds are the occasional grunts from the pigs in the neighbouring field and the excited chatter of my children. I want to make the moment last, but when, seconds later, Phoebe appears from the other end of the building calling out our names and holding up a large black key, it ends.

We follow Phoebe through the front door into a hallway paved with worn, bronze-coloured flagstones. To the left, a wide staircase leads to the upstairs rooms; to the right, a door opens into a large farmhouse kitchen. Phoebe shows us the living room with its generous fireplace and shuttered windows, then takes us upstairs to view the two bedrooms, one at each end of a long passage, and the bathroom. With each step I take I feel as if I'm leaving the past behind and marching triumphantly into the future!

The house tour at an end, we follow Phoebe through the back door to a cobbled courtyard, mostly covered in weeds but with clumps of defiant snowdrops and tiny yellow aconites. (The importance of knowing the names of trees and plants is something I learned from my father, but a conversation with Iris Murdoch a few years later will reinforce that early lesson. 'Never have your character simply sitting under a tree,' she advised. 'Have him sitting under an elm or an ash. How can you expect your readers to *see* if you don't tell them *what* to see?')

'And this is the old coach house,' Phoebe says, indicating the open building in front of us. 'Built to house two carriages, as you can see.'

'And this?' I ask, pointing to the adjoining stable door. I know what it is, but I want to hear the words. My daughter's bookshelves are full of books about horses.

'Afraid the garden is rather overgrown,' Phoebe warns, as she leads us under an archway sagging beneath the tangled weight of wild white roses. Spread before us is a walled garden dominated by a massive apple tree, with beds of flowers – and weeds! – scattered randomly through the uncut grass. 'Now if you'd come two days ago,' Phoebe informs us, 'that tree would have been covered in blossom.'

'Confetti,' I answer, pointing to the scattering of blossom at our feet. 'Just as beautiful.'

I look up at the sky, dappled with clouds, and pray to the gods, to God, that this place, with its footsteps from the past and its hopes for the future, will be ours.

* * *

Back in London I write to my mother. I have been writing regularly since I left New Zealand but I have had only one letter back. It came attached to a parcel containing a second-hand, size 40 corset, a Christmas present, the only one I ever received from her. It was signed 'Regards, Alley Somerville'. (There were never any presents for the children, nor any acknowledgement of the gifts, photos and letters I continued to send up to the time of her death. A relative would tell me, years later, that all the photos of my children were destroyed.) So I have no reason to expect my mother will respond favourably. The trustee, after his initial visit to sound her out, is not hopeful either. But I can't hold back the surges of optimism that ambush me every time I imagine myself walking through that garlanded front door.

Three weeks later the reply comes. I don't open the letter straight away. I decide to take my son to play on the Heath. If the news is bad I'll have grass and trees and water to comfort me. I walk till I get to the pond where there are benches to sit on. While my son plays with his favourite tractor I prise open the familiar blue New Zealand air letter. Clumsy by nature, I am even more clumsy this morning. I tear the letter in two. But I can see the words. They dance in front of my eyes. My mother has agreed to advance the sum we need to buy The Long House. I read the letter again to make sure I haven't imagined it. Then I say the word *miracle* out loud. Later my mother will regret her decision and insist we pay interest on the 'loan' she authorised. Later still, she will reverse this decision, writing of her 'shock' at discovering that I was 'paying interest on my own money'. But by then The Long House is ours.

# Chapter Nineteen

We move at the end of April. The plan is to arrive with as little fanfare as possible. I may not know much about village life, but I know enough to understand that we are entering a different world. What I don't yet know is that most of the inhabitants of Ascott-u-Wychwood can trace their families back to the Civil War. From Day One we are known as 'interlopers', a term applied – so one particularly taciturn villager informs me – to anyone who hasn't lived in the village since the 1640s. 'Been here since Adam played full-back for the Israelites,' he informed me, during that somewhat one-sided conversation. 'You've been here two seconds. Let's see how long you last.'

Sending the children to the village school goes some way towards mitigating our 'unwelcome immigrant' status. Children are exempt from derogatory labels. But it will be several years before I feel entitled to call myself a villager. By this time the tribe of 'uncles' and 'aunts' acquired by the children will, in the cautious way of country folk, have become part of our lives: Roly (son of gypsies) and his wife Heather (the village postie); Richard (the local builder) and Ann, whose daughter, Sally, becomes my daughter's best friend; Hazel, the postmistress, whose wartime stories I lap up like a cat with cream; Willie, the former German POW who, despite being married to a local woman (met when he was working on Crown Farm at the end of the war) is, thanks to his German-West Country accent, virtually unintelligible; Bertha, who helps me in the house, with whom I share things only mothers of sons can share; Frank, who works for Lord Rotherwick's Cornbury Estate, the largest private landholding in the district, a place that will snake its way into my fiction; Denis and Dot (Dot's pickled eggs are a village speciality) who run the local pub; Celia, who lives opposite The Long House, a crippled woman of mysterious parentage, who will cast a shadow over both a play and a novel ...

Getting to know the middle and upper classes proves less straightforward. A week or so after we arrive I'm visited by Mrs W, the Lady of the Manor. In fact, there are three manor-size dwellings in the village, but Mrs W, whose tenure goes back only three decades (as I will learn soon after our first meeting), is the one who gets invited to open the village fêtes. No accusations of being an interloper for her, apparently. Or for her husband, a sad sack of a man who seldom raises his voice above a whisper.

When Mrs W appears I'm up a ladder at the front of the house, pruning the wisteria that trails delightfully but rather too enthusiastically over our kitchen window.

'Good morning!' she calls out. 'I'm Mrs W. I've come to invite you and your husband to the annual Tory Garden Party. It's on Sunday at the Manor. We always hold it in the spring. So many people disappear in the summer.'

Clutching my secateurs I make my way down the ladder. 'That's very kind of you,' I say. 'But we're not Tories.'

Mrs W, whose head is wrapped, Queen Elizabeth-style, in a floral scarf, makes a clicking noise with her tongue. 'Oh dear,' she sighs. 'I assumed ... I'm told you own your house. Perhaps I was misinformed.'

'We own most of it,' I answer. 'The bank owns the rest.'

She sighs again. 'I was just saying to my husband this morning, we're losing far too many people to the Liberals.'

'Actually we're not Liberals.'

The answer to this is a frown and a quick shake of the head, as if to check her ears haven't deceived her. Then she says, 'Well, there's no denying there's a lot to be said for the communists. Good day to you.'

I watch her climb into her Land Rover and roar off down the street. So now we're not just interlopers, we're communists! I laugh, but can't suppress a flicker of anxiety. Have I made an enemy?

In the months that follow, Mrs W greets me with every sign of civility whenever our paths cross. On one occasion she mentions that she has heard there is a communist peer in the House of Lords. I try to tell her I'm not a communist but a supporter of the British Labour Party, but she brushes my words aside. So I tell her I know the notorious Red Peer – his name is Wogan Phillips, and he was once married to Rosamond Lehmann, whose novels I am currently adapting. She shakes her head. Clearly the name means nothing to her. For a moment I'm tempted, since she seems determined to cast me as the Village Red, to tell her about my communist cousin, Rewi Alley.

The Red label will stick, not just to me, but to my neighbours in the adjoining ends of The Long House. Phoebe, whose Roedean vowels and haughty manner belie her politics, spent much of her youth living in a left-wing commune. She would like to live communally with us. There's a blocked-up door between her studio and our front room: dissuading her from unblocking it almost scuppers our growing friendship. But then living communally would have destroyed it altogether! On the other side are Robin and Jessica, both architects, who will become close friends. Jessica's father was a prominent member of the British Communist Party, though I'm not sure how many of our fellow villagers know this. But there's no doubt The Long House is seen by many as a communist cell. When, some years after our arrival, we buy, for reasons of cost, a Russian car (I also buy a Russian piano but I take care not to advertise this), Roly, never one to let a chance to tease pass him by, seeing me with my head under the bonnet calls out, 'Talking to Moscow, are we?'

No wonder I find so few supporters when I come to set up a local branch of the Labour Party. Feudal law still applies here. Frank, who works for Lord

Rotherwick, is not the only villager living in a cottage 'tied' to the Cornbury Estate. To vote against the interests of the landowner, even in a secret ballot, is to tempt fate.

* * *

If Margaret Atwood's words are right – 'Time is not a line but a dimension' – then I have no need to apologise for the circular route this narrative is taking. I'm back at the beginning. The day of arrival at The Long House. We pull up outside our front door (badly in need of paint), Bruce driving the van we've hired, me driving the car with the children in the back. Both vehicles are stacked to the roof with cardboard boxes. I've driven the 70-plus miles from London with no rear visibility.

While the children rush off to explore, we start unloading our belongings. We don't have much – the furniture in the Hampstead flat belonged to my cousins. But our plan to slip into the village unnoticed goes up in smoke. Literally. In my eagerness to dispose of the mountain of cardboard boxes I set the living-room chimney on fire. The fire brigade is summoned from Burford and the whole village turns out to watch.

The weeks that follow are dominated by the hard work of turning a house that hasn't been lived in for months into a home. I love every minute of it. I even discover a love for gardening, though I would never describe myself as having green fingers.

On the first day of term I walk my daughter down the High Street to the village school. Not that there's anything 'high' about the street. It's a dead end, home to a mere handful of households. Back in the nineteenth century someone muddled up the signs so that Mill Lane, which should have been our address, became High Street. A drunken prank, according to legend, but no one has bothered to put it right. I've already met the school's sole teacher, a man who will be the model for the teacher in my novel *Finding Out*. Mr Stanyon, whom his pupils clearly adore, is delighted to welcome my daughter, knowing that my son will not be far behind. The school needs to keep its numbers up if it's to survive.

(This school, so central to the life of the community, will, like many others, be closed as a result of the sweeping changes – centralisation, privatisation – unleashed by Thatcher's government. It is now an Independent School. Instead of a flow of chattering children dressed in a variety of garments, many of them hand-me-down, making their way across the village green, there are Range Rovers and BMWs delivering pupils in smart new uniforms to the school gates.)

* * *

There are three villages 'under' the Wych Wood, the ancient forest gifted to the Duke of Marlborough after his victory at Waterloo but owned now by the shipping magnate, Lord Rotherwick: Ascott, Milton and Shipton. They are not fashionable. Their beauties are not on show. No tourist buses rumble along their lanes to disgorge passengers at the doors of boutique pubs serving fusion cuisine and French wine. Though The Swan, the pub that was run by Dennis and Dot (of pickled egg fame), does lay claim these days to minor gourmet status. Once a place where everyone in the village could feel at home – farm workers, landowners, retired colonels, interlopers, weekenders – it is now an establishment aimed unashamedly at the moneyed classes. Not being on the tourist trial may have protected the Wychwoods for a time, but in the end they, like almost every other village or town in proximity to London, succumbed to market forces. Most of the locals who were my friends and neighbours for more than a decade have taken advantage of the boom in property prices to sell up. These days Ascott-u-Wychwood is a village of commuters and life-stylers, few of whom have any knowledge of the dramas played out in their transformed cottages.

* * *

Our official address is The Long House, 11 High Street, Ascott D'Oyley, Ascott-under-Wychwood, Oxon. Soon after we move I discover that 'Ascott D'Oyley', the unnecessary but colourful part of our address, harks back to the time of the Civil War when the village was divided between Catholic and Protestant.

We, apparently, live in the Catholic end, a fact which takes on a retrospective significance years later but means nothing to me at the time. For a while I toy with the idea of writing about the village during the Civil War. I'm intrigued by a story told to me by Frank about the conflict between Protestants and Catholics that took the form, every Saturday night, of an actual fight on the village green for the right to use the local church on Sunday. In this part of England, the Civil War was about more than just King versus parliament. But then I hear another story, and the religious battle is forgotten.

The 'Ascott Martyrs' – the name given to the real-life characters in this new story – appear to me first as ghosts. A fellow villager, whom I encounter one morning at the post office, overhears me arranging to send money to the families of political prisoners in South Africa. Introducing herself as Eileen Pratley, she takes me aside to tell me about her great-great-aunt who was arrested and gaoled for disturbing the peace in 1873. I want to know more, but she clams up. 'It were in all the newspapers,' she informs me as she walks off. Intrigued, I take myself off to the Bodleian Library in Oxford, where I scan the newspapers for 1873: a year of vast agricultural unrest. Mechanisation is threatening the livelihood of thousands of farm workers. Where once it took eleven men to plough a field it now takes only one. A union has been formed – the Agricultural Workers' Union – to protect the rights of agricultural labourers. Oxfordshire landowners, led by the Duke of Marlborough, are incensed. There are strikes. Families are thrown out of their tied cottages. Men walk off the land, never to return ...

I know this story. It's an Oxfordshire version of the Highland Clearances. And now it's a story I want to tell.

I visit the local agricultural museum to find out what was happening in Ascott-u-Wychwood. As I suspected, the men of Ascott, like most agricultural workers in Oxfordshire, have joined the union. But their employer, the tenant of Crown Farm, is not happy. When the men refuse to renounce their membership he dismisses them and brings in blackleg labourers from neighbouring Gloucestershire. I'm getting close! The women of the village, sixteen of them, including Eileen Pratley's great-great-aunt, decide to take the law into their own hands. Carrying pitchforks, they confront the blacklegs and urge them, in 'strong, unwomanly language', to go back to their homes. All sixteen are arrested, charged with breach of the peace and sentenced to gaol with hard labour. One of the women is pregnant; another is a nursing mother.

This would have been the end of the story had it not been for Queen Victoria. Hearing of the plight of the women, she summons the Duke of Marlborough to account for what has happened. No one knows what was said in that meeting, but the outcome is an immediate royal pardon and a gift of £5 and a red flannel petticoat, paid for out of the royal purse, for each of the women. Released from Oxford Gaol, they are driven home in a horse and cart. As word spreads, villagers step out of their cottages to offer cider. Some join the procession, which will be described in the national newspapers as 'riotous' and 'unruly'. By the time the sixteen women reach Ascott-u-Wychwood, most of them are drunk.

I seek out my informant and tell her what I've learned.

'That'd be right,' Eileen says, making clear that what I've just revealed was known to her all along. 'Most of us still live here.'

Village reticence is something I'm still getting used to.

'Folk tell me you're a writer,' she goes on.

'That's right.'

'Then you'll be wantin' to talk to the descendants.'

I tell this story first as a radio play for the BBC (some of which is recorded in the village, using descendants of the original martyrs in the crowd scenes, and the children of the village school to sing the songs), then, in a different configuration, as a novel, *Riding to Jerusalem*, published in 1996. By this time the whole of Britain will have gone through turmoil similar to that which shattered the peace of Oxfordshire in the 1870s. Despite prolonged strikes and nationwide protests, thousands of coalminers, print workers, shipyard employees and steel workers lose their jobs. But in Thatcher's Britain there is no Queen Victoria to come to their rescue. The miners, the steel workers, the printers and the men who build ships have to take what's coming to them.

* * *

My relationship with the Lady of the Manor does go wrong eventually. It's 1976, the summer of the heatwave. My children, along with most of the children in the village, have taken to cooling off in the swimming hole in the Evenlode River, reached by way of an overgrown public footpath across land owned by Mrs W and her hen-pecked husband. Early one hot Saturday the phone goes. Mrs W gets straight to the point.

'I've no objection to *your* children swimming in the river,' she says, 'but I cannot have every Tom, Dick and Harry marching across our fields, trampling the crops.'

I remind her that the children are walking on a public footpath. She has no legal right to stop them. She hangs up in disgust. Next day, when the children head to the river they are greeted by a swimming hole filled with barbed wire.

I will encounter this attitude again a few months later when the local hunt comes charging through our village and one of the horses ends up trampling Frank's prize vegetable garden. When Frank comes out of his cottage to protest, the woman rider asks him in a haughty voice if he owns his cottage. Frank explains that it's a tied cottage. 'Then I'd be very careful who you complain to,' she says as she spurs her horse on to a gallop.

A decade later, Lord Rotherwick announces that the paths through the Wychwood Forest are to be closed. His reasons are commercial. He is going to lease the forest, home to partridge and monk deer, to game shooters. This is the Thatcher era. Profit rules. So the ancient, common-law right of free entry to the forest for people living 'under' it is to be overturned in favour of the rights of rich businessmen to shoot birds. I am only on the fringes of the protest movement that arises in response to this – my own life by then has imploded – but I follow events closely, finding ways, long after the successful outcome of the protest (the forest is now open to the public three hundred and sixty-five days of the year), to weave the story into my fiction.

* * *

Not everyone I encounter whose political views differ from mine stoops to the level of Mrs W. Living in one of the other 'manor' houses are a retired colonel and his wife. They don't exactly become my friends, but as our acquaintance develops there is mutual respect and even liking. Which is surprising, considering what a bad start the relationship got off to.

It was soon after we moved. I was looking for a cleaning lady. With Bruce away more often than not, keeping on top of both house and garden left me little time to write. So I decided to use my family benefit to pay for some help. The notice I put up in the post office got an immediate response. 'Mrs Stow' came to see me. She told me she lived at the other end of the village (the Protestant end!), adding that she cleaned for two other people in Ascott, one of whom was the colonel. So far so good. But then I asked her what she expected to be paid. Five shillings an hour, she answered. I gasped. People in London were paying £1 an hour. Paying less was out of the question.

'But the colonel pays five shillings,' she protested. 'I can't take more.'

'Then don't tell him.'

'Oh, I couldn't do that, Mrs. Wouldn't be right.'

Next day I received a visit from the colonel. He informed me, politely but firmly, that I was upsetting the economy of the village. He didn't actually call me a colonial, but I knew that was what he meant when he reminded me I was new to the village. I couldn't possibly understand how things worked. 'I look after Mrs Stow and her family,' he told me. 'Always have. She relies on me for that.'

'That's very good of you,' I answered. 'But I believe in paying proper wages. No one can live on five shillings an hour.'

He became angry then, though he controlled it. 'Mr Stow is a chronic invalid,' he revealed testily. 'Dependent on someone – me, as it happens – to drive him to the hospital on a regular basis. So unless you're prepared to take on that responsibility I think we should leave things as they are ...'

I watched him stride off down the High Street, a slim, straight-backed man with, no doubt, an impressive war record. A voice started up in my head: Peter

Sellers in his skit about the Lord of the Manor handing out baskets of rotten apples to his tenants. I shushed it away. The colonel was not that man.

Mrs Stow doesn't come to work for me.

So when I receive an invitation from the colonel and his wife a few weeks later, I'm not just surprised, I'm puzzled. Aren't I *persona non grata*? The invitation is for me and my husband to join the colonel and his wife for drinks on Friday. I reply, thanking them but explaining that, as my husband is away, I must regretfully decline. They respond by inviting me to come on my own.

'Don't mention politics' are the words drumming in my head as I walk from Ascott d'Oyley to Ascott Earle. Or wages. But these are political times. The oil crisis is dominating the news, as is the government's ongoing battle with the coalminers. 'State of Emergency,' the colonel pronounces when the subject, inevitably, comes up. 'Heath should have declared that from the start. Show those upstart miners who's boss.'

I can't help myself. I mention Tony Benn, whose passionate support of the miners is a thorn in the side of the government.

'Traitor to his class,' the colonel explodes. 'If he were to walk into this room now I'd shoot him.'

I look at the arsenal of guns displayed on the wall of the room and wonder for a moment if I'm going to get out alive. That I do, and remain on good terms with the colonel and his wife, is something I look back on with amazement and not a little sorrow. I'm not sure the England that made possible such tolerance and acceptance of difference exists any more.

The colonel, needless to say, would never have shot Tony Benn. Though he might not have invited him in for drinks.

# Chapter Twenty

When we move into The Long House I assume, without ever putting the thought into words, that I will live there for the rest of my life. Not since Lauriston, where I spent the early years of my childhood, have I lived in a place that feels like home. Every corner of the house is dear to me. I love the flagstone floors (a few of the stones have to be lifted to satisfy an inspector that a damp course has been installed: it hasn't – it would have destroyed the floor); the wide staircase and landing (from which, in time, we will build a mezzanine floor to house my growing library); the sitting room, where the favourite place to sit is either side of the raised hearth, close to the log fire. The window at the top of the stairs is set into an alcove from where, sitting on an old steamer trunk filled with woollen blankets from New Zealand, I can see out over the paved and perfumed courtyard – I've planted thyme and camomile – to the coach house which, following another burst of activity, will become my daughter's music room and bedroom.

After the hectic pace of life in London I've been looking forward to having time to myself, but within weeks of moving the visitors start arriving. I've long since accepted that entertaining the people my husband works with, or wants to work with, goes with the job, but now, instead of giving dinner parties, I have to entertain people for entire weekends. (Though perhaps Bruce rued the day he invited Maurice Shadbolt and his wife Bridget Armstrong to stay the weekend. 'Met them in the pub,' he explained. I didn't have to be told which pub he was referring to – The Gardener's Arms, favourite watering hole of New Zealand novelist and publisher Dan Davin and his wife Winnie, and a regular stopping-off place for Bruce on his way back from London. Dan had come into our lives when he offered, through a mutual friend, to read my first (unpublished) novel. So to me he was not just a friend, he was a mentor. Eventually he would also become my employer – I go to work for him at the Clarendon Press as a copy editor. 'Maurice seems a gloomy sort of cove,' Bruce goes on, 'but Bridget's okay.')

That weekend aside, and despite occasionally protesting at the sheer numbers that come through our door, I have to admit to enjoying a great deal of it. Our pals from Nottingham days come with their children, as do actors and directors met while we were living in Hampstead. One year I calculated we'd had only one weekend out of fifty-two without people staying. There are days when I'm too exhausted to take advantage of the children's absence at school to write.

Some of our visitors create a stir in the village. When the RSC actor Ian Holm – whom I will always think of as Troilus – asks if he can hide away with us for a few day to escape the attention he's been attracting as the star of the popular TV series *Napoleon*, the anonymity he's hoped for doesn't last. 'Guess who's staying in The Long House? Napoleon!' The news spreads like the fires in the fields at harvest time. Ian goes fishing in the Evenlode accompanied by a gang of kids anxious to show the French Emperor the best spots to catch carp ...

Of course not all our visitors are in the acting business. Friends and family members turn up on a regular basis. Some, like my Somerville cousin Gwynnedd (my kid sister in all but name) and my Alley cousin Merryl, live in the UK; others visit from New Zealand. My ex-mother-in-law, bejewelled and trailing clouds of perfume, comes to stay, as does my ex-father-in-law and his wife. When my foster parents, Margot and Angus, come for the weekend, I don't want them to leave. The same goes for friends from Auckland who arrive at the door bearing gifts – swamp kauri bowls, woven baskets, tapa cloths, Smither prints. What is going on in my homeland? Where has all this creativity come from? After they've gone I feel curiously bereft. As if the view outside my window has been temporarily leached of colour.

One friend from London who comes for the weekend leaves behind a mystery. I first met Patricia – an American with two young daughters – in Hampstead. She lived just a few doors down from us in South Hill Park Gardens. Her daughters went to the same school as my daughter. My first impression of her, which I saw no reason to change, was that she could have been a sister of Laura's: enchantingly attractive; heartbreakingly – infuriatingly! – lost in a world she kept trying to re-invent. The difference was, Patricia had money. She'd moved to London to escape the fallout from a messy New York divorce. Now, sitting at the table in The Long House kitchen, she tells me she's decided to move countries again, this time to India. She's come to say goodbye.

I'm bewildered. I can't take it in. I can hear her girls playing in the courtyard with my daughter. 'What about them?' I ask, waving my hand at the window.

'They're going back to New York. To their father.'

'But ... I don't understand. How long are you going to be in India?'

She shrugs.

'But ... but ...' Questions crash about in my head. 'Why? I thought you were happy in London.'

'I don't belong in this country. Never have. You of all people should understand that.'

'So why not go back to the States?'

'Don't belong there either.'

I look at her, and the thought in my head is that I don't know her at all. We were friends; now we're strangers.

'Do you think I could leave a trunk with your cousins? Just some personal things.'

'Mike and Carolyn?' I respond distractedly. 'I don't know. I can ask.'

'Thank you.'

'Won't you miss your girls?'

'They want to go to the States. They miss their dad.'

'You must have some idea how long you're going to be away.' I sound petulant but only because I feel I'm also having this conversation with Laura. 'I mean ... what will you tell the girls?'

She smiles. 'I've already told them,' she says. 'They understand. I'll be away as long as it takes.'

The trunk ends up in the basement of the South Hill Park Gardens house, where it stays for the next decade. When Michael and Carolyn move to a larger house in the same street, Michael writes to ask me what to do about it. I advise him to dispose of it. Patricia never kept her promise to write. I've no idea where she's living now, or even – thinking of Laura and how close she came to death – if she's alive. Michael gives me a blue vase made of fine glass, one of the items he found in the trunk. Everything else goes to a charity shop. I have that vase still.

* * *

Some of the friends who visit leave vowing to follow our lead and move to the country themselves. The actor John Hurt is the first, not that he stays for long. A man of contrasts – one person when he's sober, quite another when drunk – I think of him to this day as a devil/angel, because he seems to me to have the characteristics of both. What is not in question is his talent as an actor – one of the most exciting, if not *the* most exciting (and unpredictable) actors of his generation. He and I will work for a time on a screenplay of Elizabeth Smart's tragic love story, *By Grand Central Station I Sat Down and Wept*. In the end John decides it's not for him. 'Scene after scene of my backside pumping up and down,' he complains. 'Who'd pay to see that?'

John buys one of the three manor-type houses in the village. Parties at his house are riotous affairs, with dinner – if that's what we've been invited for – sometimes not appearing till nearly midnight. But John is more guest than host, turning up for Sunday lunches at The Long House, along with Phoebe (a regular) and whoever else is staying the weekend.

Then tragedy strikes. John's partner of several years, Marie-Lise, is killed in a riding accident.

John's decision, soon after he moved to the village, to buy two thoroughbred horses – a decision the villagers, who knew a novice when they saw one, considered a sign of lunacy – was part and parcel of his determination to embrace country life. Like most other people who came to The Long House, he was amused by the sight of our horse having to walk through the front door to get to the stable. (Subdividing old farmhouses has its drawbacks. Access to our stable, which used to be from Phoebe's end of the building, is now through our house.) To prevent the horse slipping on the flagstones, we have to lay a carpet. It just happens to be red. Perhaps the idea of having your horse walk the red carpet appealed to the actor in John.

The day of the accident there isn't just wind blowing, a storm is threatened. John, ignoring the advice of his groom, insists on going for a ride anyway. The groom, a friend of ours, urges him and Marie-Lise to wear hard hats, especially as they're planning to ride on the road. To no avail. They set out, Marie-Lise wearing a scarf, John bare-headed. They take the horses up the London road and start riding towards Chipping Norton.

I never find out exactly what happened – whether it's the wind or a passing car that causes the horses to bolt – but both riders are thrown to the ground. Marie-Lise dies soon after the ambulance arrives. John escapes with bruises and a sore head.

For a few days I'm in shock. Even the villagers, used to tragedy (you only have to look at the names on the war memorial), are silent, reserving their judgement about interlopers till John has sold up and left the village. I won't see him again until I'm living back in New Zealand. A phone call from a hotel in Auckland puts us back in touch. He's in New Zealand to make a film. I invite him to the home I share with Maurice Shadbolt in Titirangi. He arrives, bringing his own bottle of tequila and a salted glass. He and Maurice, another keen drinker, get along famously.

I never hear from him again.

**Visit**

Look up, why won't you? city refugee,
your eyes silted with the century's sadness

There's a corrugated sky, grey and gaudy red,
heavy with the day's remembered warmth

Does it oppress you, personally?

There's a rib-cage of cloud, shivering with light,
breathing up the land's dark scent

Surely that can't threaten?

Trees, silent as statues,
stare down the dying sun

What have they done to you?

Your feet tread warily, bitumen-blistered,
your hands cut at the unoffending air

'I'll miss my train,' you shout,
Or whisper, in my ear

* * *

'There is the hidden presence of others in us, even those we have known only briefly.' The more I write, the more these words of Michael Ondaatje's resonate. Even a stranger smiling at me in the street becomes, however briefly, part of me. Is that why not knowing what happens to someone you have been close to is so hard to bear? I don't know what happened to Patricia, or to Salem and Loretta, and I don't know what happened to Brenda, a friend who came into my life while

I was still living in London and was, for two decades after that, both a friend and a somewhat unorthodox mentor. A decade-and-a-half older than me, a widow with two sons, Brenda, while not conventionally beautiful, was effortlessly stylish, with a dreamy quality that drew people to her. (Rosamond Lehmann would call it 'mystery', a quality she possessed herself and freely bestowed on her heroines.) Brenda was a regular visitor both to our flat in Hampstead and to The Long House, till she too got the country bug and moved to a village in Cambridgeshire.

One of the first things I learned about Brenda was that she was interested in spiritualism and the occult. Within a very short time I was hooked. I had long since abandoned the Presbyterian Church of my youth, but not (well, not quite) the faith that informed it. If asked, I would have said I no longer believed in the God of Religion but I did still believe in God. What I meant by this was as mysterious to me as it would have been to anyone else. Now here was someone I could talk to about these inner meanderings without fear of ridicule, a woman who believed in the survival of the dead, and the God of Artists. Brenda had read and re-read Patrick White's *Riders in the Chariot*, a novel I, like her, considered one of the greatest works of the twentieth century. So when she invited me to accompany her to a séance, I jumped at the chance. This was uncharted territory for me.

The séance is held in the medium's home, an unremarkable-looking terraced house in West London. We are the only clients. We're shown into a small overheated room with a round table at its centre and chairs for us to sit on. Heavy wine-red curtains shroud the windows. The medium, whom Brenda addresses by her Christian name, is a dumpy woman in loose trousers and several layers of floaty material that make a soughing noise every time she moves. She offers us both a glass of water, asks a few innocuous questions, then begins. Almost at once her body starts to twitch, and her head shoots round as if reacting to a sound from behind the curtains. She mutters words that make no sense to me, though, from the look on Brenda's face, they do to her. A few moments later she starts to talk in a man's voice. This is not someone trying to talk like a man; this *is* a man: Brenda's dead husband, Charles.

I can't remember the details of what 'Charles' said, but it concerned Brenda's two sons, one of whom was struggling at school, and a man, also dead, who'd been in Brenda's life before she met Charles. It seems the two men have linked up in the after-life and are now joining forces to help Brenda with her problems. I have to admit I'm impressed.

On the drive back to Brenda's house in St John's Wood I ask about this mysterious other man. What she tells me is the stuff of romance. Her first job after leaving school was for a doctor famous for his work in helping set up the NHS after the war. Through him – I have to be discreet here – she meets 'the Greene boys' (her words): Raymond, a doctor; Graham, the novelist; and Hugh, the future director general of the BBC. She and the doctor she is working for fall in love. The affair that begins then lasts, apparently with his wife's blessing, for the rest of the doctor's life. When Brenda marries Charles some years after the doctor's death, it's on the understanding that no one can ever replace her first love. Now both men, according to her, are absent only in the physical sense. Their activity on her behalf in heaven is as real to her as the car she is driving.

I can see now that this was a dangerous path for me to go down, but at the time, with Brenda as my guide, it provided both a distraction from the difficulties, financial and otherwise, of my domestic and family life, and a tantalising glimpse of a happier future. I'd never quite lost my craving for a relationship that would consume me, though I'd come to accept that I was never going to find it in my present marriage. Brenda, a woman whose total lack of interest in politics or the issues of the day would have frustrated me in anyone else, understood my longings. With her I could indulge that part of myself I usually kept hidden.

I would eventually turn away from the world of clairvoyants and mediums (though it entered my life again briefly during my marriage to Maurice, who was researching the occult for a novel he was writing), but I have never been able to dismiss it entirely. Brenda never knew of my disaffection. It was not my apostasy that divided us, but illness and geography.

I learned of Brenda's illness after I came back to New Zealand. A letter from a friend of hers informed me she had been diagnosed with Alzheimer's disease. I wrote back immediately but got no reply. I wrote again. When that too failed, I tried to track down Brenda's sons. Nothing. Today I would try the internet and Facebook, but this was the early 90s. Email was still a novelty, considered by many – including me and Maurice – unlikely to catch on.

'Loss has given me a voice,' Günter Grass wrote in his essay on the New Germany, published in 1993 in *Granta*. 'Only what is entirely lost demands to be endlessly named: there is a mania to call the lost thing until it returns.'

So I call Brenda's name and the names of all those whose disappearance from my life has left sorrow in its wake, and I feel, as when a passing stranger smiles at me, that I, and they, are not alone.

* * *

**Summer Sunday**

I want to put this day down gently, lest it break.
I want to thank God softly,
lest I wake those sleeping giants whose powers
ungrace me on unrecorded, lesser days.

Nothing happened on this day –
the sun on my bare arms,
food shared with friends,
a child's gleeful crayoning across a twilight sky –

but all day long I held my breath and waited for the spell to break,
and now it's night, and on my squeezed eyes
light dances, as the bright words danced around
the table shared with friends.

An ordinary Sunday (gratefully recorded),
graced with an extraordinary joy.

# Chapter Twenty-one

Six months after we move to The Long House I'm offered an acting role. I no longer dream of an acting career, but I have, for whatever reasons, kept up my Actors' Equity membership. When I look at what I'm being offered – a small part in the Christmas pantomime to be staged at the Chipping Norton Theatre – I allow myself, for a few heady moments, to believe that this could be the springboard back into the career I've abandoned. But even as the idea takes hold, I know it's a delusion.

'Chippy', as our nearest town is affectionately known, has not had a theatre for long. The brave couple who have made it happen are strapped for cash. Unable to pay accommodation rates for big-name actors, they're forced to look closer to home for people to fill the roles. Our friend Richard, who was a witness at our wedding, agrees to direct. He casts me as the grumpy older sister of the Cinderella-type heroine. Rehearsals, usually with my children present, are the greatest fun – though with Christmas looming there are mounting domestic pressures. On Christmas Eve, having wrapped the children's presents and filled their stockings, I find myself digging leeks out of the frozen ground at two in the morning. The turkey has been stuffed, the potatoes peeled, the Christmas pudding, made back in November, released from its wrapping. The sound of my foot hitting the spade rings out in the icy silence like a stone tossed against a tin fence. I look back at my sleeping house and wonder if anyone can hear me.

Not surprisingly, being on stage again rekindles my love of acting, but the experience of juggling family life with rehearsals and performances convinces me I could only return to the profession seriously when the children were older, by which time, of course, I'd be well beyond the shelf life of most actresses. If this thought depresses me even a little, I don't remember – perhaps because I'm surrounded by friends. Richard, who directs the entire Chipping Norton season, and his beautiful actress wife Sue (of *Forsyte Saga* fame), have been friends virtually since the day I met them. Working professionally with Richard, seeing so much of them both, I feel as if I've been given a free ticket to a six-week-long party. Plus, I've made a new friend. Nicky, stage manager on the show, who lives locally and has children more or less the same age as mine, is not just a theatrical talent, she is a brilliant horsewoman with her own livery stable. Soon she will be teaching my children how to ride. When my daughter, whose passion for horses has intensified with the move to the country, shows talent as a rider, Nicky will find the right horse for me to buy. Then another connection is revealed. Nicky is the daughter of Elizabeth Jane Howard, a novelist I have read and admire. She is also the granddaughter of Robert Falcon Scott, a legend in my hometown of Dunedin, from where his ship left on that ill-fated Antarctic expedition in 1910. In the revisionist 70s and 80s, when the literary knives come out for Scott, I tell Nicky she has to go to New Zealand. There her grandfather is and always will be a hero. Eventually Nicky does come to New Zealand to attend a Scott memorial function in Oamaru. By then Scott's reputation in England has been restored, and Nicky's son and his family are living in New Zealand.

The pantomime is a huge success. I am world famous in Chipping Norton. But there will be no follow-up. To be both an actress and a mother you need, in addition to a strong belief in yourself, a great deal of help and support. I don't have that. So I turn my back on the acting world, though, through a curious turn of events, it doesn't entirely turn its back on me.

I first met Vanessa Redgrave when she came to a party at our Hampstead flat following the release of the film *Mary Queen of Scots*, in which Bruce played a small role. I liked her. Her radical views were sincerely, if illogically, held. I asked her how she could justify sending her daughters to private schools given her commitment to overthrowing the established order. She wasn't the least fazed by the question. 'I want them to have the best education this country can offer,' she answered. 'That way they will have the right tools to bring down the Establishment.'

Some months later – by which time I'm living in The Long House – I'm visited by Vanessa's brother Corin. Would I like to join the Workers' Revolutionary Party? I'm so taken aback, I say yes. I may no longer have theatrical ambitions, but I can't deny the power of the Redgrave name. I tell myself I'm already a socialist. I want many of the things the WRP claim to want: an end to private education; an equable tax system; abolition of nuclear weapons. Why not join? No one's asking me to take up arms.

I don't last long. At the first party meeting I attend, Corin asks me what I'm working on. I tell him I'm working on a novel about John Donne. This is greeted with silence. Then one of the comrades comes to the rescue.

'Okay, so you write historical fiction. We can do something with that. How about you give Donne the heave-ho, and write a story about the Tolpuddle Martyrs? You know who they are, I take it?'

I nod. Words at that moment fail me.

'If that doesn't appeal, you could always take a look at the Peasants' Revolt. Watt Tyler and co. Press any buttons?'

I've no idea what I said. Probably something innocuous that could be taken as agreement. I'm sure I didn't tell them the truth, which is that I've never seen it as my job to convert readers to a cause. I'm not an apolitical writer, far from it, but neither am I one who beats a drum for a particular set of political beliefs. When I come to write *Riding to Jerusalem*, which might have won the WRP's approval, the motivation is not political, it's personal. Since writing the BBC play the Ascott Martyrs have become so much a part of my life it's as if they, and not their descendants, are my neighbours. Telling their story in novel form is my act of homage.

So I wait for the meeting to end and, coward that I am, I send in my resignation by post.

* * *

This is the point in the narrative when I have to come clean about my Christian faith. I've touched on it elsewhere in this story, but only in passing. I realise that in calling myself a Christian I'm running the risk of ridicule. Richard Dawkins calls people mad who believe there is a mystery greater than science at work in the universe. The late Christopher Hitchens, wittiest and warmest of atheists, won almost every 'religious' debate he engaged in, with one remarkable exception. Challenged by a southern Baptist preacher in America to prove that God didn't exist, he couldn't. The preacher, on the other hand, was able to produce an impressive body of circumstantial evidence that God *did* exist. He won the debate.

But the risk remains. Being Christian is not cool. Especially in New Zealand, which is fast becoming one of the most secular nations on Earth. At the swearing in of ministers in the 2000 Labour–Alliance government, only two of the twenty-five swore their oath of allegiance on the Bible. One was Dover Samuels, Minister for Māori Affairs; the other was Deputy Prime Minister Jim Anderton, a family friend who would later become my grandson's godfather. Jim is not just one of New Zealand's finest politicians, he is a good man and a good Catholic, who knows as well as I do that he is a member of an increasingly mocked minority, asserting the validity of faith in a world that holds religion to blame for many, if not all, of its current woes.

This is not the place to mount an argument for faith over atheism, though I would say that the atheist who insists on the unassailable rightness of her position is as much a fundamentalist as the Christian or Muslim or Jew who does the same. The opposite of faith, as Pope Francis recently pointed out, is not doubt, but conviction. It's conviction that leads to those 'religious' wars for which people of faith – who are also, inevitably, people of doubt – are held responsible. Conviction is the enemy, not faith. Faith is a relationship, a way of understanding our place in the world, not a means of controlling it.

Like many of my generation I drifted away from the church of my childhood, settling back happily enough on the comfortable cushions of agnosticism. By the time of my second marriage, agnosticism had become the default position for almost everyone I knew. So how did I get from there to where I am today? It would be easy to say that my search for God began as a result of my disappointment in marriage. Easy but wrong. At the time I began seriously thinking about God I was living in The Long House. I had a home, I had children, I was a published writer: three compelling reasons to feel contented with the world. But something – and it can't be explained by my disappointment in marriage – was missing.

Enter Father Bulbeck, a Jesuit priest based in Charlbury, a larger-than-life figure (he will turn up, thinly disguised, in my fiction) whom I first encountered after he was apprehended for trespassing by one of Lord Rotherwick's gamekeepers. Dressed in his customary off-duty garb of ancient khaki shorts, loose Hawaiian shirt and panama hat, he'd gone into the forest to pray. The gamekeeper, taking him for a hippy up to no good, had carried out a citizen's arrest. The charges were dropped the moment the priest's identity was established, but by that time the story had spread to all the Wychwood villages. 'I like praying among the bluebells,' Father Bulbeck explained, when asked why he'd gone into the forest in the first place. 'They're one of God's most beautiful flowers.'

My curiosity aroused, I decide to take a look at the man for myself. I've been going with less and less enthusiasm to the local Anglican church (I'm living in the heart of Tory England: Presbyterianism is not an option), whose vicar, an unprepossessing individual, known to the village children as PG Tips, preaches the kind of rule-based Christianity I instinctively back away from. I can't blame PG for delivering me into the arms of the Catholic Church, but I can blame Father Bulbeck, at least in part. Not that he succeeded in signing me up. There were too many difficulties in the way. But for a few months after my first visit to his unprepossessing chapel in the backstreets of Charlbury, I'm a candidate.

My plan to sneak in and out unnoticed is scuppered the moment I walk through the door. I am one of a congregation of four, and the only one not to take communion.

'Welcome!' Father Bulbeck says, striding up to me at the end of the service. 'You're new here. Visiting?'

I shake my head.

'Ah ...' He beams at me. 'Hope that means you're a new resident. Our numbers' – he waves his hand at the retreating congregation – 'could do with a boost. As you can see.'

'I live in Ascott,' I mumble.

More beaming. 'Practically on the doorstep,' he says. 'So what brought you here today?'

'Curiosity,' I answer, the word slipping out before I can censor it.

He looks at me quizzically but has the good sense not to ask what I'm curious about. 'You busy?' he says. 'I make excellent coffee. I have a machine. I also make excellent beer. Though maybe it's a little early ...'

I start to make excuses – children, work, the usual platitudes – but something in his expression silences me.

That's how it started. And his coffee really was excellent. Ditto his beer, which I sampled on my third visit. As for his conversation, this turned out to be as surprising as his skill as a brewer and a barista. At first we didn't discuss God or the Church, or indeed anything to do with religion. That happened later, by which time, having learned a lot about me, we'd become friends. Of course he wanted to convert me. That was his job. But when it became clear this wasn't going to happen, there was no ill will. Our friendship endured.

It was the rules that stymied me. Particularly the one relating to divorce. 'We can get round it,' my new friend insisted. 'The Church offers a number of solutions.'

'Such as?'

'Well, if your first husband wasn't baptised, that marriage could be annulled.'

'Of course he was baptised. Everyone was back then.'

'Perhaps you could write to him ...'

'And say what? He'd just think I was having another of my crazy notions, and tell me what I wanted to hear.'

'In which case the sin would be his, not yours.'

I burst out laughing. 'That's too Jesuitical for me,' I answered him.

'There is another way...' I watched as a smile passed across his face. I suspected he knew what my answer was going to be before he even asked the question. 'You and your present husband could live as brother and sister. That way you would only have been married once, in the eyes of God.'

I don't remember what I said. I imagine I was trying not to be rude by laughing out loud again. And that was where it ended.

Father Bulbeck may have failed in his missionary role, but he left me more convinced than ever that I had to keep asking those awkward questions. When I heard he was playing an active role in the protest movement, putting pressure on Lord Rotherwick to re-open the paths he'd closed in the forest, I wasn't surprised. He may, like PG Tips, have been hampered by rules, but he didn't judge those who couldn't follow them.

So I went on being a foot-dragging Anglican, a state that lasted another two decades. In 2005 on a return visit to the village and its church, I found myself sitting next to a familiar face – David Cameron, the recently elected leader of the Conservative Party. As the MP for Witney his presence in this village, situated at the heart of his constituency, was no surprise. As we knelt together at the communion rail I was tempted to whisper, 'So it's true then. The Anglican Church really is the Tory Party at prayer.' Which would of course have been met with the contempt it deserves. By 2005 I'd met many Anglicans, quite a few of them priests, who shared my politics.

One in particular stands out: a New Zealander, born in Germany, who came back into my life (I'd known of him in Dunedin where he, like me, grew up) through his prominent role in CND. P was – is – an Anglican priest. A brilliant speaker, his sermons attracted almost as much attention as his political oratory. Listening to him was like talking with John and Shirley. The questions he raised were the questions that had to be asked, but there were no easy answers. A self-proclaimed pacifist, he freely admitted that if someone attacked his child he would fight back. Human instinct would trump any other allegiance. It would be a while before I started to write *Love and War*, but already the seeds were beginning to sprout, and the questions I had been too preoccupied to try and answer were starting up again in my head. Violence: is it innate or is it learned? If innate, is it inevitable? Would I, a pacifist by disposition, have been able to sustain that position in World War II?

Sometime after my friendship with P began I learned a disturbing fact about him. He was being watched by the British government. I can't reveal how I came by this information, but I can say the surveillance was conducted by a unit set up by Defence Secretary Michael Heseltine, referred to in the corridors of power as the 'Dirty Tricks Department'. The purpose of this unit was to dig up dirt on citizens involved in the various protest movements. P was being followed because of his leadership role in CND and his championship of a robust form of pacifism. Unfortunately P is a priest with feet of clay. He and his wife had an open marriage. They were photographed entering mixed saunas. This, plus the rumours of infidelity, were enough to discredit him and, by association, the nuclear protest movement. I passed on the information I'd been given to P, but he seemed untroubled by it. Did he want to be a martyr? Too many left-wing leaders – the Kennedy brothers, Martin Luther King – have been discredited because of their sexual behaviour. P's apparent indifference to the threat facing him disturbed me.

Eventually, for a variety of reasons, the friendship ended.

* * *

'Religion is the opium of the people,' Karl Marx declared. It is 'the sigh of the oppressed creature, the heart of a heartless world, the soul of soulless conditions'. Because it is based on illusion, it can provide only an illusory happiness. So religion must be abandoned if the world Marx imagined – to each according to his need; from each according to his ability – is to come into being. But why, I ask myself, can't we have both? Politics that prioritise those in need – whether that need be a mental or physical disability, or simply being economically and socially disadvantaged – and a religion that allows for mystery? 'And we are put on earth a little space that we may learn to bear the beams of love', Blake wrote in his poem *The Little Black Boy*. Like Marx, Blake was a revolutionary, but the world he wanted to bring into being was called Jerusalem, not Mahagonny.

I didn't want to choose. I still don't. I want to travel with both 'illusions' in my backpack.

**Unknown**

Poems about God are gifts to the godless,
for how can you know what is nameless,
name what cannot be known?

**The Love of God**

God is love.
If I loved God as I should I would see Him.
But no one can see God and live.
So I will settle for what I have –
a troubled heart that loves

# Chapter Twenty-two

It's midnight. I'm sitting on the old steamer trunk at the top of The Long House stairs, gazing out over the moonlit courtyard. The weather vane on the coach-house roof – a painted cockerel that turns with the direction of the wind – is pointing towards the garden and the fields beyond, as if directing me to look further than my own back yard. It's been a terrible week. A phone call came from New Zealand seven days ago with the news that my mother had died. She'd been in a coma for six months. The news should have come as a relief. But instead of sinking into that comforting emotion, I was hit by a tidal wave of grief. I managed to get the children off to school without visible tears, but the moment they were gone the dam broke. Bruce was at first puzzled, then irritated, then angry. 'For God's sake, Elspeth! She didn't love you. She never wrote to you. She disinherited you when you were a teenager. What on earth are you howling about?'

I couldn't explain. It would be a long time before I understood why her death affected me so violently. I understand now. I was grieving the abject failure of the relationship, and the fact that now it could never be put right. There would be no deathbed reconciliation. No gesture towards love.

I spent the rest of the day with my neighbours, Robin and Jessica, listening to the St Matthew Passion, grateful for their tactful distance and the silently proffered cups of tea. Then I took myself away for three days – the first time I'd ever done such a thing. I couldn't listen any longer to what was being said. 'Your mother hated you. Right from the start. Jealous, in my opinion. Not that you've ever listened to anything I have to say on that subject. You excuse her because she was mentally ill, but that doesn't explain why she reserved the worst of her venom for you. What you should be doing instead of filling the wastepaper basket with tissues is instructing a lawyer in New Zealand to contest the will. It's outrageous that everything's going to your brother. Where's the justice in that?'

I drove to a friend's cottage in Northamptonshire. First thing I did on arrival – it was the middle of the afternoon – was sleep for three hours: a dreamless sleep so deep that when I woke I thought I was back in Lauriston, my childhood home. For the next three days I walked and walked, following paths with no idea where they would lead, gathering mushrooms, writing lines of poetry in my head. Then I came home. Life will go on as normal, I told myself. Nothing's really changed. But somehow I knew that wasn't true. Death changes things. So does betrayal. I tried to convince myself that Bruce's dismissal of my grief was just indignation on my behalf. But that was not how it felt. It felt like betrayal. Ten years later I would discover just how far that betrayal went.

So here I am, sitting on the trunk filled with warm blankets – discarded in favour of duvets – from my homeland, thinking of my parents and my brother, picturing the wider family, gathered from all over the country, filling the Andersons Bay Presbyterian church. My parson cousin – the one who married me first time around – is reading out my telegram in which I acknowledge my mother's tragic childhood, and her courage in the face of unimaginable mental and physical suffering. I am there in my words and in my heart, saying goodbye to the woman who raised me. But when I look out the window I am somewhere else. In the time I have been sitting here, the place I had thought of as home has shape-shifted into a place of exile.

As I continue to stare out the window, seeing and not seeing the silhouetted coach house, the smudgier lines of the drystone walls surrounding the garden, the silvery fields stocked with sheep and pigs, the blur of hills in the distance,

I see my brother and my cousins shouldering the coffin with my tiny mother inside while the organ groans into life, and the spaces in my mind fill with the words I cannot speak because there's no one here to say them to. 'He who lives more lives than one / More deaths than one must die'. Wilde wrote that from Reading Gaol. So when my mother died, did she take one of my lives with her? Does that explain my paroxysms of grief? Is that the reason I'm sitting here with only the dog for company?

I make a conscious effort to come back to the present. I love it here. I'm in thrall to the stories and the people of this village. I have wonderful new friends. I look with seeing eyes across my garden to the fields. They belong to 'Harry the Milk', so called because in addition to farming he delivers milk to the village. His wife runs the local shop. Recently there was a fire in Harry's dairy, started, so the village rumour mill had it, by Pete Rainbow, the village arsonist. Harry has a temper. That he's fallen out with someone in the village is easy to imagine. That this person then hired Pete to burn his dairy down is more of a stretch. But I believe it. This is not Andersons Bay. This is Ascott-under-Wychwood. They do things differently here.

I'm about to give up my moonlight vigil when I hear a sound in the distance – a train approaching. I lean closer to the window. This is the first time I've heard a train running in the middle of the night. The sound grows louder. I turn my head and there it is, emerging out of the low hills, snaking its way across the fields towards Kingham, Moreton-in-Marsh, Evesham, Worcester Foregate Street, Great Malvern, Hereford. But wait. Something's different. This is not, as I had assumed, a goods trains. It's painted white. I shake my head. I've conjured up a ghost train. It's Cornwall, where toys were conjured up for my daughter, all over again. Only it's not. There's no magic here, no mystery to solve. The train is real. It sparkles and shines out there in the moonlight. Some weeks later I will learn why it's painted white. It's carrying nuclear waste. After that night I will see it again, twice, on other sleepless nights: a slithering white serpent threatening my garden.

* * *

**Requiem for my Mother**

The day you died I was in a house you'd never seen,
and would have hated,
with friends you'd have called
pretentious, or perhaps not even that –
irrelevant, at least to you.

I listened to the St Matthew Passion,
and thought of all that had and had not been,
of what you had seen and heard that
no one, least of all a child,
should see and hear.

And I thought of all the oceans that divided us,
and I knew this ending was all there was,
you'd never reach out now,
or hear the music played in vain for you.

* * *

## Postscript

Nearly a decade after my mother's death I am in New Zealand seeing family. I visit my brother John from whom, to my great distress, I have been estranged for the last nine years. I have no idea what caused the rift. Following my mother's death John sent me a generous cheque to compensate for my being left nothing in the will. I was touched and grateful. He didn't have to do that. But this gesture was followed by silence.

Now here I am in his house being greeted warmly by Jill, my sister-in-law, but not by my brother. Clearly the rift has not been healed. At the first opportunity

I ask my sister-in-law for an explanation. Was it something I said? Or didn't say?

'It wasn't you,' she tells me. 'It was Bruce. The letter he wrote.'

'What letter?'

'Saying you were going to challenge the will in court if we didn't send money.'

'*What*?'

She gestures helplessly. She's hating this as much as I am.

'So John thought ...' I can't finish the sentence. 'Oh God ... No wonder he wanted nothing to do with me.'

I try, of course, to explain, but why should she believe me? The money John sent was quickly spent. And I'm in no position now to pay it back. As I speak, or rather gabble, the words sound false even to my ears. I knew nothing about the letter. I would *never* have gone to court. I'd known since I was a teenager that I was disinherited. I expected nothing ... But, but – I hear the protest Jill is kind enough not to make – Bruce was my husband. I should have known what he was doing.

I don't know what my sister-in-law said to my brother, I only know the miracle (another one!) happened, and the rift was healed. By the time I return to England, John and I are friends again.

# Chapter Twenty-three

'Exile is ... terrible to experience. It is the unhealable rift forced between a human being and a native place, between the self and its true home: its essential sadness can never be surmounted ...' Edward Said's words, read after I returned to New Zealand, have stayed in my mind not because I applied them to my own 'exile' of twenty-plus years, but because my exile, while sharing some of the features Said describes, was fundamentally different. The 'crippling horror of estrangement', the 'loss of something left behind forever' which he singles out as the cruelest of exile's consequences, were no part of my experience. It's true that by the time I returned to my native land – at least I was able to, unlike the exiles Said had in mind – I no longer recognised it, but the alienation didn't last. Enough of the country I'd fled from in 1969 remained for me to find my way back.

'To have a home is to become vulnerable,' James Wood, another writer concerned with exile, has written. In his brilliant article in the 20 February 2014 issue of the *London Review of Books*, he saw that what Said was writing about was something very different from the 'soft emigration' so many of us embraced in the restless 60s and 70s. Said's 'desert of exile', Wood suggests, 'seems to need the oasis of primal belonging'. So if Wood's experience as a Briton living voluntarily in the States, and mine as a Kiwi living voluntarily in England, did not involve unsurmountable sadness, it would seem to follow that the homes we left behind could not have been 'true' homes. 'I couldn't go back home because I wouldn't know how to anymore,' Wood writes.

But I did go back home. And a reverse homesickness replaced the conventional homesickness of my exiled years. Recognising the irony in this, I began to refer to myself as a 'geographic schizophrenic' – a phrase coined by Australian writer Martin Boyd, whose works I have adapted for the BBC – a condition I have come to see as both curse and blessing. So what was different about my experience? Have I ever had a 'true' home, a place where, in the words of yet another writer on the subject of exile, Aleksandar Hemon, 'every place had a name, and everybody and everything in that place had a name, and you could never be nowhere, because there was something everywhere'? The answer to that question is yes. Lauriston, where I spent the first eleven years of my life, was home. And so was The Long House.

So where does that leave me? At the age of twenty-nine I chose to leave my native land and settle in a country on the other side of the world. It has to be one of the most important decisions I ever made, but it didn't seem that way at the time. Like choosing to marry, the gravity of the decision became clear only with the passing of time. Now that I'm living on my own in Wellington, my friends, reacting to my peripatetic life – I return every two years to England, living there for as many months at a time as I can – ask somewhat wistfully if I feel at home in my inner-city apartment. The answer is no. Those two magical houses were homes. Living in them I was surrounded by people and places with names I knew as well as I knew my own. Other places were – are – simply places to live. But I am not sad. Said describes the world of the exile as resembling fiction in its unreality. So exile can be a gift. It can even yield what Hungarian philosopher György Lukács has described as 'transcendental homelessness,' a state of being at home everywhere and nowhere.

We read in order not to feel lonely, to – in Seamus Heaney's words – 'set the darkness echoing.' All the writers quoted above have, in their different ways, echoed in my own particular darkness. I think of them as friends. Their words go wherever I go. So I do have a 'true' home, inhabited by people whose names I know, situated in places whose names I know, and that home is literature. As I type these words I am looking at a shadowy portrait, in postcard form, of Kafka, a writer I admire but have never been able to love. I used to think the words printed over his featureless face were pretentious: 'I am nothing but literature and can and want to be nothing else.' Now I think he was just building a home for himself.

* * *

The Long House was home. So why did we leave after ten years? At the time the reasons seemed compelling. I barely shed a tear as we drove away. Only now do I see that what I thought was going to be a new beginning was in fact an ending. It wasn't just our life in The Long House that was over, it was my marriage. But if whoever said 'places belong to the people who love them' is right, then the house, despite having been sold twice since our departure, is mine still, as is the village. Every time I talk of Ascott-u-Wychwood I refer to it as 'my' village.

The truth is of course that I never left. Both house and village inspire my fiction up to the present day. *Riding to Jerusalem*, the novel and the radio play, stuck closely to the facts of history, but then a contemporary event grabbed my attention (and the attention of the British press) and another story was born. Again it began as a radio play – *Who Killed Stephanie*? – which the BBC produced in 2000; then, because the story wouldn't let me go, it became a novel. *The Names of Things*, which I wrote here in Wellington, goes in a different direction from the play, but the shocking event that inspired it is the same in both stories. So far it has not found a publisher. Its problem, so my agent tells me, is that it's a literary novel dressed up as a crime novel so it falls between the cracks that separate literary from crime fiction. But writing it meant I could inhabit 'my' village again, even if the subject reminded me that all was not sweetness and light there.

* * *

While we were still living in The Long House, rumours – of incest, of arson (cue Pete Rainbow), of indecent goings-on with animals – would surface from time to time, but because they were safely outside our domain I could ignore them. If asked, I would have said they were part of the mysterious inter-connectedness of life in a village where the same families have been neighbours for centuries. The subtext, I realised, was that these were not matters for the police or social services. The village would deal with them in its own way. But then things got personal. A boy from the troubled family at the end of the High Street became obsessed with my daughter. There was a break-in at our house: photos were stolen. My daughter, then in her mid-teens, was sleeping in the converted coach house, which she loved for the independence it gave her, but after the break-in she had to move back into the main house. I didn't lay a complaint. I was sufficiently *of* the village by then to believe that a visit to the boy's father would be enough to settle things. It wasn't. The boy went on to rape a girl in the next village.

That might have been the end of the story, but fifteen years later a woman is murdered while walking her dog on one of the many paths surrounding Ascott-u-Wychwood. Vikki Thompson, a young mother of two, is a newcomer to the village, an *interloper*. She lives in one of the rash of faux Cotswold cottages that have gone up in the wake of the Thatcher Revolution. A local man is arrested. Mark Weston. I know him. He went to school with my son. I don't believe he is capable of murder, and neither does the jury. Mark is not the boy who broke into our house and stole photos – *his* name is Stuart. When Mark is acquitted, the police decide to focus on Stuart. I receive a call from a detective stationed in Burford. At the time I'm living in bushy Titirangi. Thinking myself back into the village, its houses, its re-invented school, its church, its fields and lanes, brings on an acute attack of 'geographic schizophrenia'. I tell the detective what I remember of the break-in and the conversation with Stuart's father (he thrashed his son to within an inch of his life), but he is more interested in another encounter I had with that troubled boy.

It's the late 80s. My marriage is over. I'm back in the village living in a rented cottage. My god-daughter Anna, daughter of 'Laura', has come to stay. Anna spent a year in Ascott as a schoolgirl. The Long House was a second home for her, so this is almost as much of a homecoming for her as it is for me.

It's a glorious early autumn day. We decide to take ourselves and the dog for a long walk. Everywhere we look we see acres of wheat and barley shimmering in the sunshine, pressing against the hills as if to taunt them for not producing their own fields of gold. The harvest is only days away. While the dog runs on ahead we talk about New Zealand and Anna's studies at Cambridge, and what the future holds for her. Before long we are talking about my failed marriage and the complex fallout from that. When this subject is exhausted I ask Anna how it feels to come back to the village she lived in for a year. She agrees it has changed almost beyond recognition. I don't blame all these changes on Thatcher. I point the finger at the EU too. What kind of trade deal results in the dumping in the sea of mountains of apples just because they're not the right variety? Or the killing of chickens because they don't lay the right sized or coloured eggs? (Brown is out.) Just last year a tenant farmer was ordered to slaughter his herd of prize Jersey cows, many of them pregnant, because the EU in its wisdom decided his part of the Cotswolds should farm sheep, not cows. The farmer couldn't do it. He committed suicide.

'So you don't believe in free trade,' Anna comments, raising an ironic eyebrow. 'Afraid you're in the minority. Freedom's the *mot juste* these days. Especially where trade is involved.'

'Awful, isn't it, to seem to be against freedom,' I say, 'But you have to ask yourself, freedom for whom?'

She laughs. '*Whom*? You must be the only person in the world who still says that.'

We've been walking for nearly half an hour when a shot rings out. The dog, which almost never barks, lets out a startled yelp and catapults back to my side. Anna and I look at each other. Giggle. Clearly someone's playing a joke.

'That was close,' Anna says.

'Perhaps they think we're pheasants.'

Another shot rings out. We duck for cover. I grip the dog's collar. 'Shush!' I hiss at him.

'That was *really* close.'

I raise my head slightly. There has to be an innocent explanation. We're on a public footpath. We're surrounded by wheat. Or is it barley?

'Hey!' I yell. 'Whoever you are, stop shooting. We're not birds.'

The third shot sees us both on our feet and running for our lives. The dog dashes ahead, comes back to check on us, dashes ahead again. I take Anna's hand, then let it go and tell her to run on. She's twenty-five years younger than I am. Anna grabs my hand back and refuses to let go. In the blur of running I see a figure with a balaclava over his head, moving in parallel with us along the lower end of the field. A nervous giggle turns into a cry. This is surreal. This doesn't happen in the Cotswolds on a hot afternoon with insects buzzing and swallows doing cartwheels overhead.

At last we reach Pudlicote, a hamlet of fewer than a dozen houses. We burst in on the first house we come to. It happens to be Pudlicote Manor, a somewhat grim building surrounded by high walls which I long ago decided was an MI5 training site, since no one with a name appeared to live there. Knocking on the door, too breathless to speak, I experience the first real flash of panic as it occurs to me the place could be deserted. It can only be a matter of minutes before Balaclava Man catches up with us.

Our faces must have told a story, because the moment the door opens we are pulled inside. Our rescuer is an old man with a whiskery face and clothes that hang on his bony frame like washing. We explain as best we can, two voices stuttering out a tale of what we are only just beginning to grasp was attempted murder. The old man picks up the phone. An agonising wait, during which we drink the strong tea our rescuer has made for us, ends with the arrival of the police.

Over the next few days a lot of questions are asked, but while I – and the police – believe the culprit was Stuart, he, thanks to his sister, is able to provide an alibi. Recently released from prison, Stuart has come back to the village to live. According to the police he's convinced I had something to do with his arrest for rape. 'There's the motive,' I say to Anna.

So did Stuart murder Vikki Thompson? I'm not the only one who thinks so. But we will be proved wrong. A decade and a half after his acquittal, Mark Weston is arrested again (the law of double jeopardy was changed in the UK in 2005). New evidence has been found linking him directly to the crime. He is currently serving a life sentence.

* * *

When rumours become facts, perceptions change. A threat to my daughter was a more than sufficient motive to sell up and go. But there were other, more nuanced reasons. Both my children were at school in Oxford, twenty-seven miles away. The commuting by train and bus worried me far more than it worried them, but then came a winter's day when the temperatures dropped to minus 12 and snow covered the land. This was not picturesque snow, with apple-cheeked children tobogganing down hills and timely scatterings of salt on the roads to keep the country moving. This was a whiteout. Not even the dog would step outside the door. He knew how quickly you could get lost in a world without visible markers.

The phone rings. It's my son. He's lost his way in Oxford. Having started to walk from the school to the station (buses have stopped running), he has become completely disorientated. I tell him to stay in the phone box, urging him, as calmly as I can, to jump up and down to keep warm. I want to keep him on the line, but I have to ring the police. I'm trapped in the village. Who else is going to rescue him? I tell the woman PC who answers how long my son has been walking and where I think he might be, but my heart is beating so fiercely it's affecting my speech. 'Is there anyone he can stay with in Oxford?' she asks. 'Trains aren't likely to be running again for at least twenty-four hours.' I give her the name of my closest Oxford friends and urge her to hurry. I can see my son, minus his coat – which, on past form, he will have left at school – shivering and miserable in that icy phone box. Three days later, when he finally makes it back to the village, I begin to listen to the arguments for moving.

Acting work has dried up for Bruce. Jobs are offered, but they're rejected: 'Two lines in a biblical epic no one'll go and see? You've gotta be joking. Didn't travel twelve thousand miles to put a tea towel on my head …' He's convinced a move to Oxford will re-ignite his career. He'll only be an hour from London. Meeting people – networking – will be that much easier. Besides, The Long House is now worth a lot of money. If we sell we can pay off our debts, make a fresh start.

But there are other reasons. Things have gone sour in the village. It's not just the problem of Stuart. Bruce has fallen out with a number of people. All of a sudden the village is full of 'inbreds' and 'snobs'. There's no question of apologies or making amends. My husband doesn't do sorry. His solution to the problem is to move. Already he has his eye on a property in Oxford: two cottages that he plans to turn into a single dwelling. As the son of a builder he knows what he's talking about. I've recently started working for the Oxford Playhouse, reading scripts. Two of my own plays – *The Body Politic* and *Consequences* – are scheduled for production there. 'You'd be on the doorstep,' Bruce points out, upping the ante. 'You could walk to work.' I remind him I do all my reading at home, but it's a feeble argument. Once rehearsals start I will be needed in the theatre every day.

The ground has started to shift beneath my feet.

# Chapter Twenty-four

The Long House is sold on a wine-filled evening in February 1982 over the long refectory table in our kitchen. The buyer is our accountant, Michael. (Bruce and I had always had a joint account and shared finances. But in the run-up to the decision to sell, when I discovered the extent of our debts, I opened an account of my own, figuring I would have more chance of putting food on the table if I kept control of my earnings. Bruce was outraged. With no sign of irony, he insisted that it was illegal for married women to have their own accounts.) Michael is paying for the house in cash. A paper bag containing hundred-pound notes is passed across the table. He is paying us the market price – £50,000. If I was concerned about the unorthodox nature of this transaction I have no memory of it. Michael was a larger-than-life character, an accountant (so we believed) to many famous people in the world of theatre, film and television. Four years later when our paths crossed again I would discover he wasn't an accountant at all, merely a defector from the tax department. When I look back on that night in The Long House and replay the scene around the table, I wonder how I could have been so gullible. It was a scene straight out of a gangster movie: the paper bag stuffed with cash; the flow of drinks. My naivety will cost me dearly.

So now it's time to sell the horse, pack up the books, take down the Smithers and the Binneys and Cook's map of New Zealand, and say goodbye to the village. I tell myself I'm not really leaving, just moving closer to my children's schools and to my work. I've recently changed agents. I didn't fall out with Deborah, just slipped too far down the food chain. My new agent, Diana Tyler, will not only advance my BBC career, she will take on the novel I have just finished – *Finding Out*, set on the Otago Peninsula of my childhood – and sell it to Random House. I tell myself the move will mean I can see more of Diana. It will be good for *my* career too.

Despite the £50,000, and the comparatively low cost of the two Oxford cottages, we are desperately short of money. The trustee has made it clear there will be no further advances. My half of the trust has been spent. Our safety net is history. So once again we do the move ourselves, hiring a van and making repeated trips to Oxford till The Long House is nothing but a shell. Even now I can hardly bear to think of it. Not only am I leaving a house and a village I love, I'm leaving friends. Little Tew, a mere half dozen miles away, is home to the writer Peter Buckman and his beautiful literary agent wife, Rosie. Their family life is so closely entwined with mine I cannot imagine living apart from them. Closer still is Charlbury, home to actor Freddie Jones, his actor wife Jennie and their three gifted sons. Condicote, a short car ride away, is where Nicky and her family live. These places are not just names to me, they're emotional signposts.

But the most difficult parting of all is with my friend Carole. Carole arrived in Ascott a few years after we did, turning up, like Mary Poppins, to put things right in my world. That I should find a soul mate in this Cotswold backwater still strikes me as miraculous (that word again). A single mother with a son the same age as my own son, Carole is Jewish, secular, compassionate, highly intelligent, and will soon be fêted as the author of two brilliant biographies, of Jean Rhys and Primo Levi. With our shared obsession with literature and writing, it's hardly surprising we became friends. But there is another element. Ever since I stumbled, as a very young child, on the horrible truth of what the Nazis did to the Jews, I have been drawn to the Jewish culture and its people like a moth to a flame. I'm not sure if what I feel is guilt – I'm not a Jew: I belong to the tribe who persecuted them – or anxiety. Would I have had the courage to hide my Jewish friend in my house?

For months after I get to know Carole I have a recurring dream. I'm sitting at my desk in The Long House when I hear an angry knocking on the door. I know who it is – the Gestapo. I've hidden Carole in a secret compartment in the wall of the house. (Only now do I realise where this image of the hidden compartment comes from. I'd assumed it harked back to the priest holes I'd been shown when researching *Catch a Falling Star.* Now I have another explanation. Holidaying as a child with Great Aunt Clara, mother to Rewi, at the Alley family home in Christchurch, I stumbled on a concealed passage with its own secret door. A lifetime fascination with hiding places was born.) In my dream I open the door. Two men in long overcoats and trilby hats enter. They start questioning me. That's when I see the key to the compartment lying in plain sight on the floor. I try to move my foot to cover it, but I'm paralysed. I wake in a sweat.

I would probably still be having this dream if I hadn't, on impulse one day, told Carole about it. She looked at me for a moment, then she shook her head. 'Why the anguish?' she said. 'Do you think I'd have hidden you if the roles had been reversed, and we, the Jews, were top dog? At least you hid me. I might not even have done that.'

But I know Carole *would* have hidden me. This is a woman who fights for the rights of Palestinians, and has given shelter and support to refugees through her voluntary work with Asylum Welcome. She would not only have hidden me, she would have defied the Gestapo. That's the kind of woman she is. I never had the dream again.

Of course I will still see Carole. That's what I tell myself as we join the traffic on the London road. As I will my other friends in Little Tew, and elsewhere. Oxford is not alien territory.

My diary for 1982 gives no indication of the turmoil that surrounded our departure from The Long House, it simply records the date. 'Move' it says. Practised at persuading myself that what is necessary is also good, I tell everyone who asks that this seismic change in our lives is a 'good thing', of benefit to us all.

No more commuting for the children. No more being stranded in snow storms. I will be in walking distance of the Playhouse and of the Clarendon Press (where, thanks to Dan Davin, I am currently employed as a copy editor). Bruce can go to London every day if he wants. How can the move not be good?

Would things have been different had we not moved? Would the marriage have lasted? The answer to the first question is yes; to the second no. Though I didn't know it then, and would resist knowing it for too long, the foundations on which the marriage was built were already eaten away. Perhaps there had never been a foundation. Perhaps it was all in my head. It's possible that if we'd stayed in the village the sense of belonging, of being at home, would have continued to blind me to the reality under my roof. But it couldn't have blinded me to the mounting debt, not once I'd seen the figures. I had never been blind to my husband's fecklessness with money, but I had made a decision not to let money be an issue in our marriage. Compared to him, I had had a comfortable, even privileged, upbringing. As a socialist I welcomed the chance to even the score. Besides, I had a bulwark against poverty in the form of my father's Trust. A dozen years later, all that money was gone, exposing the fault-line that had been there from the beginning. Bruce never forgave me for taking control of my own money. Two years later, when he told me he was in love with someone else, it came as no surprise to discover the woman in question was wealthy.

After everything falls apart I come back to Ascott-u-Wychwood for a short time to live in rented cottages. But I can't afford to buy at the rapidly rising prices. If I want my own home I will have to look elsewhere. 'Every traveller wants to find the place where being what he is will matter, and that place is home,' my friend Robert Dessaix wrote in his beautiful novel *Corfu*. I don't know how much I mattered in the village, but my former neighbours greeted my return, brief though it was, as if they had known all along that I would be back. Walking my dog across the familiar fields, watching him chase rabbits (he never catches them), crouching by the Evenlode River with my arm around him, both of us with a wary eye on the swans who are nesting, I see my story for what it is – a tiny ripple in the water, no different from all the other ripples, all the other stories of loss and failure – and I am for those few brief moments at peace. 'All shall be well ... And all manner of things shall be well': words I didn't know at the time, but which seem now to describe the feelings that so often overwhelmed me under Cotswold skies.

Years later, living with Maurice in his house overlooking the Manukau Harbour, the sounds of tūī and myna birds in my ears, I will read Vidia Naipaul's brilliant novel (which is really an autobiography), *The Enigma of Arrival*. Maurice has just finished reading it. He's declared it to be one of the best novels he's ever read. I had read most of Naipaul's fiction by then and been deeply affected by it, but when I met him at a friend's dinner party I changed my opinion of him. He may be a brilliant writer, but he's arrogant. And he doesn't like women much. Those were my impressions. So I start reading reluctantly ...

Naipaul is living in a cottage on the Wiltshire estate of Stephen Tennant (the model for Evelyn Waugh's the Hon. Miles Malpractice, as well as for Cedric Hampton in Nancy Mitford's *Love in a Cold Climate*). At first he doesn't really take in his surroundings. He's too absorbed in his own work. But gradually he stops seeing what's around him as frozen history, and starts to see the myriad daily changes that happen in a rural landscape. Curious, he begins to explore the nearby village and the lanes and paths that wend across fields and into woods. Slowly, imperceptibly, as he walks in 'the wild garden and the orchard beside the water meadows', his 'stranger's nerves' are soothed and a feeling he describes as peace possesses him. He has come to England with his own particular history; now England has come to him.

*The Enigma of Arrival* is the perfect and complete expression of what it means to live in voluntary exile. It is also the perfect and complete expression of what it means to fall in love with the country you have chosen to live in. I wish I'd written it. Because it describes the peace I found walking beside rivers that might have provided fish to my French-speaking Somerville ancestors, following ancient paths across fields trodden by royalists and roundheads, and farmers whose names would have been known to Shakespeare, straying into the Wychwood Forest, like Father Bulbeck, to look at the bluebells ...

I would not find that peace anywhere else.

* * *

'Places belong to the people who love them.' So I keep returning to Ascott-u-Wychwood because I never really left. Recently I wrote a novel for children set partly in Ascott and partly in Stow-on-the-Wold, where I lived after the period of renting came to an end. The novel was written for my grandchildren, the elder of whom was twelve at the time and, like most of her contemporaries, more interested in her iPad than in books. Rather arrogantly I hoped my book might change that. I had written only once before for children – a version of the stories I used to tell my son each night: *The Remarkable Adventures of Ib Ob and Uncle*. My agent took that first book on, but it never found a publisher. Not that this deterred me. I was a mother. Of course I knew how to write for children. How wrong I was. My granddaughter was kind about the book, but instinct told me it hadn't hit the mark.

So I turned to two friends, both experts in the field, and they, with considerable tact and kindness, put me on the right track. Twelve-year-olds, I learned, expect a bit more grit than I had put into my story of a lost cat. When the book was finished I sent it to my agent. To my surprise she agreed to take it on. Whether it finds a publisher or not is almost irrelevant because of the joy I experienced writing it. Searching for the missing feline – as my two main characters do – meant I could wander with them down the shadowy, tree-lined lanes and paths of the Cotswolds. I could climb the small hills, cross the stone bridges and dip my toes into the reedy waters of the Evenlode and the Windrush. I could smell the meadowsweet choking the edges of the fields, and listen to the melancholy chatter of crows and jackdaws, drowning for a space of time the constant keening of pigeons. I could hear the haunting sound of church bells on Sunday and think about the God of my childhood, and the God I was still seeking. I could lie on my back and look at the clouds scudding across the sky, and be at peace.

# Chapter Twenty-five

Our new home – 31 West Street, Osney Island – is, for the first few months quite literally a hole in the ground. The plan to combine the two dirt-cheap, rundown terraced cottages we've bought has met a hitch. The cottages have no foundations. The problem reveals itself the moment the floorboards are lifted. Both cottages are poised over water. Officially we're living on solid ground, but as I stare into the watery abyss at my feet the impression I have is that this is not a house, it's a leaky houseboat.

Thanks to the enthusiasm of the Victorians for bridge-building, Osney Island, site of an eleventh-century monastery that was home to the nuns of St Frideswide, is technically no longer an island. But it feels like one. Bordered by the River Thames and a backwater stream known as Osney Ditch, it provides ample scope for boaties and (in the case of my children) for swimmers brave enough to dive off the Botley Road bridge (an activity that has since been banned). It is also prone to flooding. The two cottages that are now our home were built to house railway workers. Presumably, since the larger managerial houses on the island were built on solid foundations, railway workers were deemed undeserving of such luxuries. I shudder to think of the damp-related diseases that must have flourished in these waterlogged cottages.

Having discovered the extent of the rebuilding required, we adjust as best we can to an existence typified by strange river smells, clouds of thick red dust, the daily presence of sweaty men in overalls, awkward negotiations to get to the upstairs bedrooms, and meals cooked and eaten on the edge of a six-foot cavern, at the bottom of which foul-smelling water swishes and swirls. At first Bruce is actively involved in the work, but as the hole slowly fills up and something like normality is established, he begins to lose interest. By the time the floor is laid and the two cottages are more or less one, he's stopped working on the house altogether. Acting work – the kind he is prepared to accept – has dried up altogether. After a brief period of being debt free, the bills start mounting again. The men in overalls leave. Work that still needs doing is left unfinished.

At the end of our second year in Oxford, Bruce flies to New Zealand to work on the film *Other Halves*, a job he is at last willing to accept.

* * *

Six months after the move to Oxford, with bankruptcy looming, I take a job that pays better than my part-time employment with the Clarendon Press and the Playhouse. John Man, an Oxford-based writer, hires me to work with him on a ghost memoir, something I had never imagined myself doing. The book that resulted – *A State of Blood* – earned well, staving off the threat of bankruptcy. The subject of the book, Henry Kyemba, was a former cabinet minister in Idi Amin's murderous Ugandan government. In order to interview him safely, John and I had to be housed, much to my children's delight, in an MI5 safe house. The weeks that followed will forever be associated in my mind with the thrill of being 'in danger'. (Amin did send an agent to assassinate Henry, but his identity was so obvious the police picked him up at Heathrow and sent him straight back to Kampala.) It was an exciting time. Each day I would bike along the canal to the safe house in North Oxford where I would listen to the horror stories of life in Amin's Uganda and try to turn them into a cohesive story. Later I would work with John on two other 'ghost' books – *The Siege of Mogadishu* and *The Survival of Jan Little*. Writing to order may not sound like the best career move, but I learned a lot working on these books. I learned to think quickly, to make snap decisions when two equally appropriate words or phrases occurred to me. And I learned not to take myself too seriously.

* * *

At this point – I'm going back here, to the time before Bruce is offered the film in New Zealand – another word appears, cryptically, in my diary: 'lawyer'. The initial appointment is made by Angus and Margot during a brief visit the year after we move. Margot makes no secret of her dismay at what she is seeing. The house is habitable, but only just. The workmen have gone. Bruce's mornings are spent reading the paper till the pub opens at eleven, when he disappears. Angus, inclined at first to be sympathetic – as a former soldier he's seen male depression before – changes his mind when the £5 note he left on the kitchen table for my son disappears. 'Saw Bruce pocket it on his way out the door,' he tells me. 'What sort of man steals from a child?'

'Just talk to the lawyer,' Margot urges on our last evening together. 'See what your options are. What if Bruce never works again? How will you manage?'

* * *

The day Bruce is due back from filming in New Zealand, I wake feeling as if someone has poured concrete into my veins. For a few terrified moments I believe I am actually paralysed. Sun is pouring through my window – *our* window. It's a beautiful June day. Bruce's flight is due at eleven. I can't move.

I don't remember getting out of bed or anything else about the morning except for the dress I wore: one of two cotton shirt-dresses, red and green, bought in a sale. I choose the green one. Green is the Catholic colour of hope, though I didn't know this at the time. Perhaps if I'd worn the red one (blood and fire) the day would have unfolded differently.

My mind is empty as I drive away from Oxford towards Heathrow. I see but don't see the blur of traffic, the looming road signs, the litter-embroidered trees lining the roadsides. I've met Bruce so many times after long absences – at train stations, airports, waiting for the sound of his car to pull up outside the house – but I've never felt like this, so heavy I have to fight the urge to slump over the wheel.

I park the car and head for the terminal. The plane is on time. Bruce is one of the first passengers to emerge. He takes his hand off his trolley and waves enthusiastically. Next minute he's beside me, engulfing me, his beard scratchy against my cheek, his voice (which I always loved) whispering in my ear. I notice how well he looks. And something else. He's not usually as effusive as this.

'You look great,' he says, more than once. 'I've missed you.'

'How was the flight?' I ask as we head towards the carpark.

'You know me,' he answers, grinning. 'Nothing I like more than free booze and a good movie.'

'You must be exhausted.'

'Slept like a baby.'

'You know I've got this do later. The publisher's party.'

'That's why I flew back today. The family wanted me to stay, but –'

'I was going to say we don't have to go. If you're shattered, I mean.'

'Course we're going. It's why I'm here. Not every day you get a chance to meet an ex-prime minister.'

'There's no guarantee we'll actually –'

'You know, Elspeth, you're your own worst enemy. Your publisher invites you to an exclusive cocktail party to meet Harold Wilson, and you want to cry off. No wonder you're not –'

'Not what?'

'Never mind.'

We get to the car. Bruce wants to drive. I'm happy to hand over. He's been drinking on the plane but he's not drunk. This is not one of the occasions when I have to wrestle the keys from him.

He starts talking as soon as we've exited the parking building. Bruce is a good talker, but I've never known him quite so voluble. It's as if he wants to tell me everything that happened while he was away, starting from the very first day.

There's no need for me to question him about the filming, or about my friends, who are now, of course, his friends too. Names, places, dates – they all come pouring out.

As I listen, I ask myself why my body is still in such rebellion. This is what I've always loved about Bruce's homecomings – the stories, the jokes. So why, when he's sharing his adventures in even greater detail than usual, has the heaviness not left me?

Approaching Oxford, Bruce suddenly takes a detour.

'Where are we going?' I ask.

'Something I have to tell you,' he says, his voice changing with the change in direction. 'Thought we could have lunch at The Perch.'

He doesn't speak again, other than to order lunch, till we're seated in the garden of the pub. I don't often see a vulnerable side to Bruce, but I see it as he walks across the garden, carrying the tray with our food and drinks. It's nothing I can put my finger on. He isn't stooped. His hands aren't shaking. But it's something I will see again when we are no longer together, and I glimpse him by chance in the street or on a train.

'Something happened in New Zealand,' he says, after we've sat in the murmuring summer silence for a few moments. 'I know you'll understand when I explain. You're such an extraordinary woman. You understand things other people would ... well ... might anyway ... freak out about.'

I raise my eyes. A lone swallow is carving an arc in the sky above me. Its white breast flashes like a butterfly wing against the vast blue of the sky.

'You remember Judy?' Bruce says. 'The Judy I was engaged to before I left New Zealand.'

'Your mother told me about her. You've never ... You broke the engagement when you got your scholarship. That's what your mother told me.'

He looks puzzled for a moment. 'My mother didn't like her much. I'm sure I talked to you about her.'

I shake my head.

'Well, anyway, I bumped into her. In the street. Queen Street as it happens.

How corny is that? But then you know what they say about New Zealand. Two degrees of separation –'

'What happened?'

'We had coffee. As you do. Got talking. Then –'

'You had an affair,' I say for him.

A sound comes out of his mouth that isn't a word, but there's no mistaking what it signals – relief. 'Knew you'd understand,' he murmurs.

I look up, but my swallow has gone. The heaviness is still there, but it's been overlaid by a sense of calm. A warm summer's day. Lunch in a pub. What could be more normal?

'Actually … I wouldn't call it an affair,' Bruce says.

I reach out to touch his hand. I don't know why. I'm so calm now, if I closed my eyes I'd fall asleep. I look around the garden. My eye is caught by a man and woman at the table nearest the river. They are talking intently while their toddler plays at their feet. Aren't they worried he'll fall in?

'More like honouring the past,' Bruce says.

'Honouring …'

'We would have married if I hadn't gone to England.'

'Why didn't you?'

'Oh … you know … I was going to be a student again. Wouldn't have been much of a life for her.'

'So you broke it off.' I sound calm, but there's a new feeling now. Nausea. 'Is she beautiful?' I ask.

He looks stricken for a moment, then he says, 'She's married.'

'Oh …'

'It's not happy. The husband's a cold man. A control freak.'

'Do they have children?'

'Two. Grown up, more or less.'

'I imagine the husband's rich. A rich businessman …'

'Look … I know what you're thinking, but it's not like that. *She's* not like that. You'd like her, Elspeth. She's good fun. And she's … you know … like you.

A good person.'

'Did you tell her your marriage wasn't happy?'

'Course not. That wouldn't have been true. I love you, Elspeth. You're my wife. This isn't about ending anything.'

'Then what is it about?'

'I told you. Honouring –'

'The past. Yes ... So it's over, then. That's what you're saying? You won't be seeing her again. Writing to her.'

He drains his beer. 'Something else I have to tell you,' he says.

I stare at his face. I'm like the clairvoyants I used to visit, staring at the cards, or the runes, or the lines on my palm. Staring, and staying calm, and feeling sick.

'There's a good chance ... well, better than good actually ... that I'll be playing a major role in a TV series to be shot in New Zealand over the summer. Their summer. It would mean –'

'Living there,' I say. 'With Judy.'

'She's going to leave her husband,' he says, clearly relieved that once again I've articulated his thought for him. 'Been wanting to for years.'

'And now she's got you, she can do it.'

'She knows all about you. That I don't want to lose you. I told her what an amazing woman you are. That if anyone could understand it would be you.'

'You're going to live with us both ...'

Bruce laughs. 'Well, not at the same time, but ...'

'Of course. She'll have money. Unlike me. No-fault divorce. Isn't that the law now? Split everything down the middle?'

Bruce frowns. 'I'm not marrying Judy, Elspeth. I'm married to you.'

'But you're hoping to get work in New Zealand. A TV series. It's what you've always wanted. Work that would lead to –'

'Things have changed out there. There's a lot happening. And with Australia so close –'

'The sky's the limit!' I look at my watch. It's twenty past three. School will be out. 'We need to go,' I say.

Bruce takes off his glasses and rubs them on his handkerchief. I recognise the signs. He beckons to the waitress clearing a nearby table. 'Another beer, love,' he calls out. 'Same again,' he adds, as she reaches for his glass. 'It's Morrels.'

'We have to go,' I repeat.

I wait for the beer to come, and the inevitable cigarette to be smoked, then I get to my feet. To my relief, Bruce follows. I didn't have a plan B if he'd insisted on staying. But the need to get away, to be somewhere else, *with* someone else, is propelling me out of my seat, out of this poisoned garden. I'm afraid I'm going to throw up ... which I do, to my own and everyone else's disgust, in the carpark.

In the car I listen to Bruce's voice, but I can't make sense of his words. He doesn't want me to say anything to my friends in Auckland. He's worried about Judy, her reputation. 'You know what a hotbed of gossip the place is,' he says. 'So until her divorce is through –'

'What?'

'Just for now,' he says. 'Thing is' – and he names three friends from my university days – 'they don't know that Judy and I were ... Not that we *were* really ... But for Judy's sake I'd prefer it if they went on thinking we were just old mates who'd got in touch.'

'So why tell me about it? If no one else knows.'

'Well ... there's always the chance someone might ... you know, say something to you ...'

We reach home. I'm forced to make a dash for the bathroom. Bruce goes for out for a 'quick drink'. When he returns he looks at his watch and asks me why I'm not dressed for the party. 'I'm not going,' I tell him.

'*What*?'

'Upset stomach.'

He steps back. His expression is one of irritable disbelief.

'You go. My invitation will let you in.'

I can see he's tempted, but instead of arguing he shakes his head, and turns away.

The rest of the day, like the days and weeks that follow, passes in a haze. I spend a lot of time in the bathroom. Bruce spends a lot of time in the pub. For five months we live under the same roof. Outsiders would see very little change in our daily routines. I escape whenever I can to spend a night with Carole, or with Angy, wife of John Man, who has become a close friend. Bruce takes advantage of my absences to host dinner parties. On one occasion I return earlier than expected to find the house full of people I don't know. Bruce, rising to the occasion, spins a yarn that not only explains the situation, it has everyone laughing.

Eventually I walk out. Bruce stays on in the house. The children (my daughter is at university by this time), the dog and the cat come with me. Eight months later Bruce finally agrees to sell. By then he has moved in with Patricia, a wealthy widow and near neighbour, two decades older than he is. When that relationship collapses, he moves in with the recently widowed Winnie Davin.

The New Zealand work never eventuates. Had it done so, Bruce would presumably have gone to live with Judy, not with Patricia or Winnie. But the relationship with her continues long distance, fuelled by Bruce's occasional visits, till he moves in with his last partner, Sarah, who has a house in Putney, and Judy is sidelined.

(Years later I will meet Judy at a literary function she has helped organise in Auckland. It takes me a few moments to comprehend what this attractive woman, who has asked to speak to me, is saying. 'Would you like me to leave? I'll understand if –'

'You're Judy!' I splutter.

She bites her lip. Distress is written all over her face.

'*The* Judy.' Impulsively I throw my arms around her. 'Course I don't want you to leave,' I say. Bruce told me I would like her. He was right. There's something transparent about the way she's looking at me. I want to tell her I bear her no ill-will; that she was not the cause of my marriage ending, only the occasion. But this is not the moment. When the formal part of the evening is over I look around for her, but she's gone. I never see her again.)

* * *

I have no diaries for 1985 or 1986. I can't account for this. I must have had appointments to keep, people to see. Did I throw them away? If I did, imagining that such an action would help me forget what was going on, I can only say the ruse was unsuccessful. I may not remember the sequence of events, but I remember how it felt to live through those months when the ground under my feet turned to quicksand.

For most of that time I simply drift. I rent first one then another cottage in Ascott, trying to keep up a semblance of family life, seeking solace in the familiar paths and friendly faces, the warm stone cottages and cold Norman church. With no diary to tell me the where and when of events I have to rely on memory, that 'robust reality' which, according to Vladimir Nabokov, makes 'a ghost of the present'. But while the memories are vivid, the sequence of events is blurry. By 1987 I am living in a two-bedroom terraced cottage which, apart from a small mortgage, is all my own. It's in Stow-on-the-Wold, not far from where Nicky, who found the cottage for me, has her livery stable. I am no longer drifting physically. But I am not at home.

* * *

**Frost Over Oxford**

What is there to do but rage at the beauty of this day,
Its meaning forever out of reach?
Something in the way the light falls, or earth receives it –
each brick and stone a jewel,
colour heightened to scarlet or gold,
edges sharp and particular as
fine lines drawn in unrefuted proof –
makes me feel an intruder.

It's the hour after dawn.
Each object has its aura.
Whited windows hung with crystal, a
thread of smoke suspended between earth and sky,
a line of poplars burning at the city's end.

It's too early to bear witness.
At the point where the light stops my head turns to stone.
Trees cluster darkly. Their shadows seep like bruises on the
white skin of the land.

Inside my head a gong is sounding,
eyes twist against the cold.
Look! A solitary heron flings itself at heaven,
wings embroidering the edges of the town.

In the space between the day and its meaning
I hurl my unredeeming words –
'In the beginning
In the beginning
In the beginning ...'

# Chapter Twenty-six

The cottage in Stow-on-the-Wold is tiny, only two bedrooms. Family life goes on but it's not the same. I test the waters of the local Anglican church but I feel like a leper in their midst. Are these the people who voted Maggie Thatcher back for a third term? If so, what on earth am I doing sitting among them? Unemployment stands at over three million. Sectarian violence continues on an almost daily basis in Northern Ireland ... I start reading about Stow and discover a terrifying history of feudal exploitation and misery. 'Stow-on-the-Wold / Where the wind blows cold / And the cooks have nothing to cook ...' as the old rhyme says.

I am trying to find my 'way through the world', something the poet Wallace Stevens tells us is more difficult than 'the way beyond'. I am not succeeding.

* * *

It's a time for writing poems. Dozens of them, many that end up in the trash bin.

It is also a time for lovers. There are two, both actors; both, in their different ways, beautiful men. But the 'way through the world' stays closed.

**The Kiss**

When you kissed me your lips were moist.
I took it as a sign.
Numberless days of ordinary life passed.

Now I'm by the sea, an inland dweller,
parched, beached, a kipper in a box.

When you kissed me your lips were moist.

Suddenly I'm drenched in spray,
scales fall from my eyes,
waves of light burst inside my head.

When love grows cold there is hell to pay,
sighs the kipper in the box.

But you kissed me, and your lips were moist.
I'll take it as a sign.

* * *

It is also a time for work. There is no help for me and the children from Bruce. And there are debts. Bruce persuades our bank manager that we are reconciled, and borrows a further £4000 on the joint account I thought I had closed down. The bank manager tells me I should have come into the bank and signed the appropriate forms: a phone call was not enough. Later I will discover other debts, some of them involving people close to me. Eventually I decide to change my name by deed poll. If my legal name is no longer the same as Bruce's, perhaps the letters demanding payment will stop landing on my doormat. So I become Elspeth Sandys not just professionally but legally.

Towards the end of my first year in Stow I receive a letter from a friend in

Auckland asking if I would be interested in applying for a job being advertised in Continuing Education. The position is for a single term only, teaching creative writing to graduate students. Knowing my situation, my friend thought I might be interested. My heart lifts. I have no thoughts of returning to New Zealand permanently, but this would earn me some much-needed cash and give me a break from dealing with the ongoing stress of the separation. My daughter is away at university, my son is at a weekly boarding school in Thame, twenty miles east of Oxford. Could they take him as full-time boarder for a term? The answer is yes. I write back to my friend. By the middle of December the job is mine.

Then comes what in film language is called 'the reversal'. Early in the New Year I receive a letter from Her Majesty's Revenue and Customs (HMRC), summoning me to a hearing. I have been charged with submitting a false return. The words swim in front of my eyes. How can this be happening? In the past all our joint dealings with HMRC were handled by Michael, but since the separation I have been managing things on my own. What did I do wrong? I declared all my income, claiming only for writing-related expenses and as sole parent to my son. In my panic I phone Michael. I've hardly said a word before a string of abuse comes down the line. I'm a *pathetic bitch*, a *miserable failure*, a *fucking killjoy*. 'Bruce said you'd never agree to it,' he snarls.

'Agree to what?'

'That he claim to be supporting you and the boy in return for paying your increased tax bill.'

'I don't understand ...'

'Bruce is a fool. He should have talked to you about it.'

'I still don't ...'

'The job in America. You knew about that, I assume.'

'Of course, but –'

'Paid well. Bloody well.'

'He told me it was only one episode. Not much money in it at all.'

Michael snorts. Or laughs. Hard to tell which. 'All you have to do is tell those idiots at Revenue that you made a mistake when you sent in your return, and Bruce is supporting the whole damn lot of you. You'll be fined, but it'll be a drop in the ocean compared to what you'll save Bruce in tax. You can do that much, can't you? You won't be out of pocket. Bruce'll pay whatever's owing.'

When I say no, it unleashes another round of swearing, at the end of which he slams down the receiver.

I stare at the phone in horror. What do I do now? Eventually I pick it up again and phone my lawyer. He advises me to get myself an accountant. If it comes to legal proceedings he will act for me, but an accountant should be able to sort it out. Later that day my agent Diana phones. I tell her what's happened. She has an idea. Why don't I talk to the accountant who handles the agency's affairs? The next day I meet Harry, who agrees to become my new accountant. A series of semi-comic events follows. Harry puts in a request to Michael to hand over all the papers relevant to the hearing. Michael refuses. A security firm is hired to force the issue. Michael continues to resist. There's a scuffle, and Michael is arrested. He spends a night in a prison cell. Harry duly delivers the evidence to HMRC and the case against me is dropped. But by this time the job in New Zealand has gone to someone else.

* * *

Looking back without the aid of diaries, I'm forced to invent a chronology to give some shape to the confusing events of that time. But one thing I can date for certain – the day I started working for Ben Kingsley. It was shortly before Bruce went to New Zealand. Ben, who'd become a friend when he was working with Bruce at the RSC, hired me to write a script based on the life of John Donne. Since his starring role in the film *Gandhi* (my children christened him 'the handy bendy Gandhi'), Ben is in a position to dictate the work he does. He's read my novel on Donne and was sufficiently impressed to take me on as a scriptwriter for the production company he has set up. Every day I drive to his house near Stratford and we talk through ways in which the story might be told. Ben doesn't want a linear narrative à la *Gandhi*; he wants to get to the heart of the man. I am in complete agreement. I'm not yet able to articulate my thoughts about the circular nature of time and the ways in which events buried in the past can have consequences years later, but I am sufficiently disenchanted with the beginning, middle and end structure of storytelling to be excited by what Ben is proposing. When he suggests filming in a walled garden where different aspects of Donne's life are displayed, I begin to see what a unique film this could be. We agree on the premise – Donne, who famously posed for a deathbed portrait, is dying. As his mind wanders back over his life, he travels around the garden, reliving his key experiences ... I couldn't wait to get started.

Then things go wrong. Bruce returns from New Zealand and the marriage starts to disintegrate. I will never know what happened, but between one day and the next I'm sacked and my script is returned to me. Bruce, at the time of the separation, visited Jane, the BBC producer with whom I'd worked on the Rosamond Lehmann adaptations as well as other plays, telling her a tale that put the blame for the failure of our marriage squarely on me. Apparently I had become paranoid, imagining affairs where there were none. (I would have the same experience years later when married to Maurice Shadbolt.) Fortunately Jane decides to check with me and an important professional relationship and friendship is saved. I can only think that Bruce told a similar story to Ben, and on that occasion was believed.

* * *

Ben had been paying me handsomely. Had the work gone on, it's possible I would have been able to buy my way back into Ascott-u-Wychwood. But I couldn't dream my way out of this situation. I have no choice but to look for a regular job.

The first one I take on is so demoralising I become a putative chocoholic just to get through the days. My employers are rich Americans who've bought an antique shop in Stow-on-the-Wold. Their interest in genuine antiques is as fake as most of the goods in their shop, some of which have been deliberately 'damaged' to make them look old. As I wait for customers to come in through the door, it's as if my younger self – the naïve young woman who tried and failed to sell shoddy floor cleaners to housewives in London – has come back to haunt me.

Eventually, having sold almost nothing, the Americans give me my marching orders.

My next job is more congenial. The new owners of the Chipping Norton Theatre, where I made my brief return to acting, hire me to run their publicity. I last a week – not because I'm sacked, but because Diana lands me a contract with the BBC that will keep me in considerably more than shoe leather for the next year. I am to work with writer David Spenser on a twenty-three-part radio adaptation of Galsworthy's entire Forsyte oeuvre. The story will not stop with Soames and Irene and Fleur, as the famous TV series did, but go on to take in the next generation. It will prove to be the most successful classic serial the BBC has ever produced.

By the time the series is being recorded I've left both Stow-on-the-Wold and England, but I return to work in the studio with some of the finest actors in the country: Michael Hordern, first encountered in Nottingham, plays Old Jolyon; Alan Howard (a friend from Hampstead days) plays Soames; Amanda Redman is Fleur; Diana Quick a radiant Irene; Rachel Kempson, mother of Corin and Vanessa Redgrave, a delightful Aunt Hester; my friend Angela Pleasence plays June; another friend, Fiona Walker, plays Winifred. The narrator is Dirk Bogarde, whom I will forever associate with *Ill Met by Moonlight* and the Cretan resistance. He's not very good. Radio is an unfamiliar medium for him, and the director is too in awe of him to tell him he doesn't need to use so much voice. But no one complains when the series goes to air. The audience figures are through the roof.

* * *

Hope, Václav Havel has declared, is 'a state of the mind not a state of the world ... It is not the conviction that something will turn out well, but the certainty that something makes sense, regardless of how it turns out.' Living in Stow-on-the-Wold didn't make much sense to me while I was there – my children were leaving home, my faithful dog and cat were growing old – but I see those five years now as a necessary bridge between my life in England and the life I would lead when I returned to New Zealand. It was not a happy time, but neither was it a hope-less time. I had my friends, I had my work, and I was still a citizen of the world. I went on protesting, in London, in Upper Heyford, believing that protesting against nuclear weapons, against the misuse of American power, against the wholesale closing of mines and print-works without thought for the future of the tens of thousands of workers involved, made sense – even if it didn't lead to a better world in my lifetime. I'm not sure we know any more what to protest about, or to whom. I only know that hope has to be a 'state of mind' before it can ever become the 'state of the world'.

**Ordinary Things**

I love the ordinary things of life –
headlights in the autumn mist and
dry leaves crackling underfoot,
the way water brims in rivers after rain and
people walking home from work and
streetlights coming on.
Love first light and ticking clocks,
and the sliding off of sleep.
Love men in pubs and kids on bikes,
and women coming out of doors to check up on the street.
Love the moon in all its moods,
and stars when God allows,
and cups of tea poured just in time to
restore my failing powers

# Chapter Twenty-seven

**High Plane Humming**

High plane humming in an English sky,
why do I feel you as threat?
Ether-blue, unconscious afternoon,
you offered me oblivion, but this

intrusion shocks. Out of the blue
fall pieces of the puzzle whose shape I'll never know.
Born in war, parents unknown,
blinded by ancestral darkness.

High plane humming over English fields,
twelve thousand miles away, how was I
involved?

I wrote this poem in Stow-on-the-Wold on a soft summer's afternoon when the air was perfumed with the scents from my tiny garden and the nose-tickling smell of the meadowsweet that decorates the town's verges. I could hear the bustle from the marketplace where another busload of tourists was being encouraged to admire the Old Market, drink warm English beer in the Queen's Head Inn then venture, if they were in the mood to spend ridiculous amounts of money, into one of the genuine antique shops. The unlucky ones would walk into the shop where I used to work and, for a similar amount of money, buy a fake antique.

Was I already thinking of going 'home' when I wrote this poem? Apart from when I considered going to Auckland to work for a term, I don't remember consciously thinking that my time in England might be over. I was still in love with the country, though not with Stow-on-the-Wold. My daughter, who'd spent her pre-university gap year in New Zealand, had decided that that was where she wanted to live, but my son remained committed to his life in England. Not to mention the friends I believed I couldn't live without. Plus I had work. The Galsworthy contract was a lucrative one. Would the BBC still employ me if I lived 12,000 miles away?

Early in 1989 something happens that seems not so much to provide an answer to the questions I've been asking as to make them go away. I receive a letter from Maurice Shadbolt. Since I know now that 'time is not a line but a dimension', this letter belongs with the weekend a decade earlier when Maurice and his wife Bridget came to stay at The Long House on Bruce's invitation. At the time there was nothing unusual about this: as a regular at the Gardener's Arms, favourite watering hole of Dan and Winnie Davin, Bruce would often come home with news of the 'Kiwi mafia', expats as well as visitors. The more celebrated the people he encountered, the more enthusiastic his report. Writers, artists and academics on sabbatical were drawn to the Davins' witty conversation like tūī to the kōwhai. After a few beers Bruce would start issuing invitations for weekends at The Long House.

The visit of Maurice and Bridget fell into that category, but whereas I have forgotten many of those exhausting, exhilarating weekends, I have not forgotten this particular one. Even had it not taken on such retrospective significance, it is probable I would remember it anyway. Accompanying the adults was Maurice's daughter Brigid (the difference in spelling is crucial), whose mother Barbara would, in twenty years' time, displace me in Maurice's affections. Brigid (known as 'Little B' to distinguish her from 'Big B'), was the same age as my son. I credit her indirectly for the good impression Maurice made on me. I saw him that weekend as a devoted father, an opinion I would revise when I went to live with him. It's not that he was *un*loving, more that it was the *idea* of his children he loved. The reality, for the most part, was too much for him.

Despite the clarity with which I can recall the visit of Maurice and his family, I can't for the life of me remember where they slept. The coach house was still unconverted so we didn't have a spare room. Usually, when people stayed, the children doubled up to make a room available. But Maurice plus Big B plus Little B makes three. Did they sleep in Robin and Jessica's house, as often happened when our generous neighbours weren't in residence? My mind is blank. What is not blank, what is in fact so vivid it's as if it happened yesterday, is what Maurice says when he follows me into the garden, smoking his pipe (reminding me of my father), fixing his incredible blue eyes on me.

'You are the person I should always have been with. If I'd been with you from the start I would still be with you.'

I stare back at him. Where did this come from? Bruce and Bridget are back in the house. The children are playing in the village playground across the road. I have no idea how to answer him.

'What are you doing here anyway? You don't belong in this country. You belong with me, in New Zealand.'

I laugh (at least I hope I did). 'For the record, I love it here,' I protest. 'It's my home. I'm happy.'

'In your marriage? No, you're not. Anyone can see that.'

'But I *am* married, Maurice. And I have children.'

'I can see you in my house in Titirangi,' he goes on, ignoring my words but not my eyes, or my hand, which he is now holding. 'You'd love it. Surrounded by bush, overlooking the Manukau Harbour. It's the perfect house for a writer. The perfect place.'

I remind him he's married too. In fact he's been married to Bridget for only a year. But this seems to make him even more determined to convince me I'm in the wrong place with the wrong man.

'What you don't know is that I fell in love with you years ago,' he says, with every sign of sincerity. 'When you were an actress. I saw you on stage at the Mercury. You were Jessica in *The Merchant of Venice*. I went backstage to talk to you, but I lost my nerve. You were surrounded by people. I was too shy –'

'And who were you married to then?' I ask.

'Gill. But it was over. We weren't even living together … Listen to me, Elspeth. I mean every word I say. You've always been there, in my mind, in my heart. The other women, the wives, they were all substitutes for you.'

They leave late on Sunday, but it doesn't end there. There are letters. There's a lunch in London. I feel guilty agreeing to meet him, but I can't resist. To matter so much to someone is heady stuff. Years later I will learn that the words which drew me into his orbit were not original. He'd used them before. A friend from university days will tell me that he used the same formula to persuade her to give up her singing career and go to live with him in the bush. She was also the woman he 'should always have been with'. He'd seen her on stage and fallen in love with her. She didn't belong where she was (Australia), she belonged in New Zealand, with him.

Six months after the weekend at The Long House, Maurice and the two Bs return to New Zealand. Maurice continues to write, but gradually the letters change, wooing giving way to literary chat (we happen, for a time, to share an agent), complaints about the marriage, and the difficulties he's having with his current writing project. After a while I stop replying.

So the letter that drops on to my doormat in Stow-on-the-Wold on that chilly February day comes as a complete surprise. I don't have the letter now. In a fit of pique, on discovering yet another retrospective infidelity (I was living on my own by this time), I decided to burn all Maurice's letters, and would have done it too were it not for a chance conversation with Michael King, who persuaded me the letters had value. On his advice I took them to the Alexander Turnbull Library where, to my gratified astonishment, I was offered rather a lot of money for them. So I can't quote the letter that changed my life, but I do remember clearly Maurice's expression of surprise that Bruce and I had separated (we'd been apart five years, but apparently the news had only just reached Titirangi). Maurice wanted me to know that he and Bridget had also separated. He didn't say how long they'd been apart, but the implication was that it was many months, if not longer. In fact, as I would discover much later, Bridget was still living with him in Titirangi when he wrote the letter. When I eventually arrive at the house that will be my home for the next eight years, many of her possessions, including her piano, are still there.

As I read the letter with the familiar name on the back, my heart starts to race. By the time I've reached the end – Maurice has written on an aerogramme; signed it with passionate expressions of love – I've lived through an ending (of my life in Stow) and a beginning (of my life with Maurice). I know this is foolish. I can recite all the things that are wrong with it: 'too rash, too unadvis'd, too sudden'. But I can't stop my imagination carrying me off to a place I feel I've been shut out of all my life: love (the kind that lasts); a home (the kind that doesn't get sold). Maurice is a writer. He's not an actor or a man burdened by family expectations. He's like me. He lives with words. I see us talking over candle-lit dinners, arguing about the world's greatest writers, supporting each other's stories, loving each other's children.

Six weeks later I put my cottage on the market. Maurice has bombarded me with letters and phone calls. I know it's for real now. His voice at the end of the line is soft and seductive. I believe him when he says he's shy. He's promised me we can live anywhere in the world. So long as we're together he doesn't care where it is. I'm not giving up England, I tell myself, I'm joining it to New Zealand. 'Places belong to the people who love them.' Maurice understands that, and accepts that I belong in two places – my native land and the country I adopted. I have nothing to fear.

I arrive at Auckland airport on a bright October afternoon. Maurice is there to greet me. I see him before he sees me – a thin, stooped, grey-haired man on the threshold of old age. The Maurice who wooed me ten years ago in England was dark-haired, handsome in a brooding, Dylan Thomas way, with piercing blue eyes. That is not the man I am looking at.

He's seen me now. He's walking hesitantly towards me. Is he aware how much he's changed? Is he worried I might reject him? He wants my love, but what he has at this moment, as his arms reach out to me, is not love but compassion.

* * *

'Without loss there would be no literature,' Günter Grass wrote. 'People without a homeland have broader horizons than those who live where their fathers and forefathers did.'

I'm not living where my fathers and forefathers lived, I'm living in Titirangi, a suburb of a city I never liked, where I was once very unhappy. But I've learned something in the months since I left England. I've learned that the real loss is not of a place or of people, but of the sense of wonder we are all born with – Wordsworth's 'clouds of glory'. As we grow older and become obsessed with securing a place in the world, that glory fades, as Wordsworth knew all too well. Wonder is replaced by anxiety.

But the memory of wonder remains. It's what unites us to one another. It's what drives the impulse to make music, to dance, to paint, to sing, to write. It's the reason I will find myself, years after I leave Stow-on-the-Wold, re-imagining my time there, writing a story about a missing cat for my grandchildren. I wasn't happy in Stow, but that was because I didn't allow myself to see it, just as I never allowed myself to see Auckland when I lived there. So I'm going to try to be happy in Titirangi; to turn my back on anxiety; to stay connected. This is my home now. The vertiginous slope on which Maurice's house is perched, the bush that creeps in under doors and windows, the constantly changing skies that curve into the sea are all, if I look hard enough, bathed in Wordsworth's 'celestial light'. 'Thanks to the human heart by which we live, / Thanks to its tenderness, its joys, and fears, / To me the meanest flower that blows can give / Thoughts that do often lie too deep for tears.'

* * *

Last night, at home in my flat in central Wellington, I had a dream that stayed in my mind long enough for me to write it down. I'm walking on a dirt track under a sky that gives no clue as to where I am. No seagulls or swallows or tūī to hint at a location. The track is wide, with a double indentation that suggests it might once have been a farm track. But the tyre marks are buried under grass and weeds. No vehicle has passed this way for a long time. Though I can't identify where I am – the Otago Peninsula? the hills behind Lake Wanaka? the Cotswolds? the path between Talland Bay and Polperro? – I feel calm, even happy. I'm barefoot. The grass tickles my toes. Ahead is my destination, as unknown as my present location, but I'm not afraid. I'm supposed to be on this track. I'm happy to go wherever it takes me.

**Resurrection**

My head is full of sky.
I've pushed up through a density of earth –
mud, flood, stones, bones,
tangle of weeds, roots,
dead branches, fossil-strewn –
through even the sea's drowned silence into
light.

Not spring, not yet –
snowdrops, crocuses, the pretty, poisonous aconite,
champagne bubbles on a bursting tide –
but my spring, mine,
  my swallow-swoop, jet-streamed across the sky,
  my prayer pearl plucked from the dark rock's side,
  my death denied.

# Quotation sources


p. 11 Jenny Diski, *In Gratitude*, Bloomsbury, 2016.

p. 12 Enoch Powell, *Joseph Chamberlain*, Thames & Hudson, 1977.

p. 13 Andrew O'Hagan, in 'Ghosting Julian Assange', *London Review of Books*, March 2014.

p. 13 Philip Roth, *Deception*, Simon & Schuster, 1990.

p. 19 Ted Hughes, *Poetry in the Making*, Faber & Faber, 1967.

p. 27 Julian Barnes, *Staring at the Sun*, Jonathan Cape, 1986.

p. 43 Karen Joy Fowler, *We Are All Completely Beside Ourselves*, Putnam, 2013.

pp. 65, 68 and 157, Oscar Wilde, 'The Ballad of Reading Gaol', in Harford Montgomery Hyde, *The Trials of Oscar Wilde*, Dover, 1973.

p. 69 Margaret Atwood, *Surfacing*, McLelland & Stewart, 1972.

p. 76 quotation from Foreword by Judi Dench in John Bailey, *A Theatre for All Seasons: Nottingham Playhouse: The first thirty years 1948–1978*, Nottingham Playhouse, 1994.

p. 82 Saul Bellow in *Letters by Saul Bellow* (ed. Benjamin Taylor), Viking, 2010.

p. 95 Kate Grenville, *One Life*, Text Australia, 2015.

p. 100 Ted Hughes, *Poetry in the Making*, Faber & Faber, 1967.

p. 109 Walter Benjamin, *On the Concept of History*, 1940.

p. 128 Margaret Atwood, *Cat's Eye*, Virago Press, 1990.

p. 140 Michael Ondaatje, *Divisadero*, Knopf, 2007.

p. 153 *Blake's Poems and Prophesies*, J.M. Dent & Sons, 1954.

p. 161 Edward Said, *Reflection on Exile and Other Essays*, Harvard University Press, 2002.

p. 162 Aleksander Hemon, *Blind Jozef Pronek and Dead Souls*, Doubleday, 2002.

p. 163 *Diaries of Franz Kafka*, Schocken Books, 2009.

p. 172 Robert Dessaix, *Corfu*, Picador, 2001.

p. 173 V.S. Naipaul, *The Enigma of Arrival*, Viking, 1987.

p. 173 Jukan of Norwich, *Revelations of Divine Love*, Martino Fine Books, 2013.

p. 184 Vladimir Nabokov, *Speak Memory*, Victor Gollancz, 1951.

p. 187 Wallace Stevens, *Wallace Stevens: Collected poetry and prose*, Library of America, 1997.

p. 192 Václav Havel, *Disturbing the Peace: A conversation with Karel Huizdala*, Vintage, 1991.

p. 200 Günter Grass, *Peeling the Onion*, Houghton Mifflin Harcourt, 2006.

p. 200 William Wordsworth, 'Ode: Intimations of Immortality', from *Recollections of Early Childhood*.